TWAYNE'S WORLD AUTHORS SERIES

A Survey of the World's Literature

GERMANY

Ulrich Weisstein, Indiana University

EDITOR

German Expressionist Poetry

TWAS 543

GERMAN EXPRESSIONIST POETRY

By ROY F. ALLEN

University of Duisburg

TWAYNE PUBLISHERS

A DIVISION OF G. K. HALL & CO., BOSTON

Copyright © 1979 by G. K. Hall & Co.

Published in 1979 by Twayne Publishers,
A Division of G. K. Hall & Co.
All Rights Reserved

Printed on permanent/durable acid-free paper and bound
in the United States of America

First Printing

Frontispiece woodcut by Max Pechstein for the Expressionist
broadsheet anthology of poetry and prose, *An alle Künstler! (To
All Artists!* 1919), which was circulated during the post-war revo-
lutionary period.

Library of Congress Cataloging in Publication Data

Allen, Roy F   1937–
German expressionist poetry.

Twayne's world authors series ; TWAS 543 : Germany
Bibliography: p. 145 - 53
Includes index.
1. German poetry—20th century—History and criticism.
2. Expressionism.   I. Title.
PT553.A4   831'.9'1209   79–493
ISBN 0-8057-6386-4

to Barbara
with all my love

Contents

About the Author

Roy F. Allen was born in St. Louis, Missouri in 1937 and educated in the public schools of Southern California, at UCLA (B.A.) and the University of Wisconsin (Ph.D.). He has held teaching posts at the University of Illinois-Urbana, the Technische Universität Hannover, the University of Vermont and is currently teaching at the Gesamthochschule Duisburg. He is the author of *Literary Life in German Expressionism and the Berlin Circles.*

Preface

Expressionism is now (in the mid-1970's) experiencing another great renascence of public interest, one that is already proving to be much more intense than that of the late 1950's and early 1960's. Symposia on Expressionism and retrospective exhibitions of Expressionist art are taking place in many cities in Europe and the United States. Numerous studies of Expressionist literature have appeared in print and many others are in preparation. A large part of the literature of the movement is being reissued in reliable reprints. All this activity has been inspired by more than specialists; Expressionism seems more topical today than at any time since the Expressionist era itself (1910–24). Expressionistic ideas, themes, styles, and techniques are still alive in contemporary art and literature (very prominently in the "Young German Cinema" movement). And read as history, we can learn much from Expressionism to help us — as contemporary Americans and Europeans — to understand our turbulent and troubled times. For Expressionism represented an artistic response to an age profoundly similar to ours, marked by the emergence of the great twentieth-century political powers, whose industrial and technological might was threatened and challenged — from within by disaffected intellectual, economic, and racial minorities and from without by new, developing nations, struggling to survive and maintain their own identities. Thus, in looking back on Expressionism, we can certainly better understand what is happening to us now and perhaps even anticipate some of what lies ahead. To gain such insights is, after all, one of the primary purposes in studying literature, or studying history of any sort.

The present analysis is an attempt to assess, for the general reader as well as for the specialist, the poetry of German Expressionism. There are several reasons for concentrating on this genre. First of all, a large number of full–length studies of Expressionist drama have appeared in German and English since the 1920's. The drama has also been reassessed in several major studies in the last decade or so. Even the prose of the movement has recently been given its first broad critical treatment. Expressionist poetry, on the other hand, has not been dealt with in a comprehensive work since World War II, and never before in English. This is quite surprising and regrettable. Poetry was the first literary genre to emerge from the Expressionist movement. Poets, such as Stefan Zweig, Peter Scher, and Hugo Kersten, who identified with the movement early on, recognized at its outset that a new "age of the lyric" was dawning. In fact, poetry was clearly the dominant genre in the early phase of Expressionism (1910-14). Of the attention devoted to literature in the many activities sponsored by the Expressionists in this period (publications' of journals, almanacs, anthologies, and volumes in series; recitals in cabarets, salons, and clubs; aesthetic campaigning and theorizing) the most extensive was given to the lyric poem. While the Expressionist drama was later to dominate the critical interest of the public, it did not actually reach its heyday until near the end of the movement's second phase (1914-18). Expressionist prose — because of its length and its inability to sustain the tone of excitement that is so crucial to the life of a movement — remained a decidedly secondary genre.

A word about the translations is necessary. In deference to the general reader, all poems cited in the text are given both in the original German and in English translation. All translations are by the present author, although several of them benefited from the work of Michael Hamburger, one of the very few translators who have made substantial efforts at rendering this difficult poetry. The aim of the present translations was to convey the essential meaning and tone of the original as faithfully as possible, not always literally but rather in American English of an equivalent stylistic level which is readable as verse. The reader must consult the original for subtleties of meaning, vocabulary, meter, rhyme, syntax.

There are many people to thank for their very kind and generous assistance in the completion of this study; space limits mention here to only a few. I wish to thank, first, the Graduate College of the University of Vermont for generous grants in support of the research for this study; also the staffs of the libraries of the Schiller-National museum, Marbach a.N. and of the University of Vermont for making important materials accessible. And I wish especially to express my gratitude to my wife Barbara for her moral support and encouragement as the research and writing of this study progressed, for her valuable assistance in the very difficult translations of Expressionist poetry and for her patient help in the typing of the final manuscript. Last but not least, I am grateful to Professor Ulrich

Preface

Weisstein for his meticulous and expert editing of this study in its final stages.

ROY F. ALLEN

Gesamthochschule Duisburg

Acknowledgments

Acknowledgment is gratefully extended to the following for their kind permission to quote copyrighted material:

to the Verlags AG "Die Arche," Peter Schifferli, Zurich, for "Karawane" from Hugo Ball, *Gesammelte Gedichte,* ©1963; for "Die Dämmerung" from Alfred Lichtenstein, *Gesammelte Gedichte,* ©1962;

to the Aufbau-Verlag, Berlin and Weimar, and the Limes Verlag, Wiesbaden and Munich, for "Ewig im Aufruhr" (excerpt), "Klänge aus Utopia" by Johannes R. Becher from *Menschheits-dämmerung: Ein Dokument des Expressionismus,* ed. Kurt Pinthus, Ernst Rowohlt: Hamburg, ©1959; "Vorbereitung" (excerpt) from Johannes R. Becher, *An Europa: Neue Gedichte,* Kurt Wolff: Leipzig, ©1916, rpt. Kraus-Reprint: Liechtenstein, ©1973; for "Päan des Aufruhrs" (excerpt), "Familie," "Gesang vor Morgen" from Johannes R. Becher, *Verfall und Triumph,* vol. 1, Hyperionverlag: Berlin, ©1914, rpt. Kraus-Reprint: Liechtenstein, ©1973; for "Aufruf zum Neuen Mensch" (excerpt) from Johannes R. Becher, *Gedichte für ein Volk,* Insel-Verlag: Leipzig, ©1919, rpt. Kraus-Reprint: Liechtenstein, ©1973;

to Edwin Bohne, Berlin, in behalf of Eva Kanehl, for "An Alle" (excerpt), "Revolution" (excerpt) from Oskar Kanehl, *Die Schande: Gedichte eines dienstpflichtigen Soldaten aus der Mordsaison 1914-18,* Verlag der Wochenschrift Die Aktion: Berlin-Wilmersdorf, ©1922, rpt. Kraus-Reprint: Liechtenstein, ©1973;

to Verlag Helmut Küpper (formerly Georg Bondi, Düsseldorf), Stuttgart, for "Komm in den totgesagten park und schau" from Stefan George, *Das Jahr der Seele,* ©1964;

to Rudolf Zech, Berlin-Friedenau, for "Fabrikstädte an der Wupper: Die andere Stadt" (excerpt) from *Deutsche Grossstadt-lyrik vom Naturalismus bis zur Gegenwart,* ed. Wolfgang Rothe, Philipp Reclam Jun: Stuttgart, ©1973;

Acknowledgments

to Irene Kowaliska-Wegner, Rome, for "Des Dichters Lied von den Dirnen" (excerpt) from Armin T. Wegner, *Das Antlitz der Städte,* Egon Fleischel: Berlin, ©1917, rpt. Kraus-Reprint: Liechtenstein, ©1973;

to Prof. h.c. Kurt Heynicke, Merzhausen, for his "Aufbruch" (excerpt), "Mensch" (excerpt) from *Menschheitsdämmerung: Ein Dokument des Expressionismus,* ed. Kurt Pinthus, Ernst Rowohlt: Hamburg, ©1959;

to Limes Verlag, Wiesbaden and Munich, for "Nachtcafé" (excerpt), "D-Zug," "Der Sänger" (excerpt), "Alaska," "Das Plakat" (excerpt), "Synthese" (excerpt), "Reise" (excerpt), "Gesänge" (excerpt) from Gottfried Benn, *Gesammelte Werke,* ed. Dieter Wellershoff, vol. 3, ©1963; "Trieb," "Wunder" from August Stramm, *Das Werk,* ed. René Radrizzani, ©1963; for "Erscheinung" (excerpt), "Weisheit" (excerpt), "Der Idealist" (excerpt), "Meine Zeit" (excerpt) from Wilhelm Klemm, *Aufforderung,* Verlag der Wochenschrift Die Aktion: Berlin-Wilmersdorf, ©1917, rpt. Kraus-Reprint: Liechtenstein, ©1973;

to the Ernst Rowohlt Verlag, Hamburg, for "Weltende" by Jakob van Hoddis, "Der politische Dichter" (excerpt) by Walter Hasenclever from *Menschheitsdämmerung: Ein Dokument des Expressionismus,* ed. Kurt Pinthus, ©1959;

to the Verlag Heinrich Ellermann, Munich, for "Der Aufbruch" (excerpt), "Form ist Wollust," "Reinigung" (excerpt), "Der Spruch" from Ernst Stadler, *Dichtungen,* ed. Karl Ludwig Schneider, vol. 1, ©1954; for "Ophelia" (excerpt), "Der Gott der Stadt" from Georg Heym, *Dichtungen und Schriften,* ed. Karl Ludwig Schneider, vol. 1, ©1964;

to Ellen Otten, Locarno, for "Thronerhebung des Herzens" (excerpt) by Karl Otten from *Menschheitsdämmerung: Ein Dokument des Expressionismus,* ed. Kurt Pinthus, Ernst Rowohlt: Hamburg, ©1959;

to Otto Müller Verlag, Salzburg, for "Kaspar Hauser Lied," "Ruh und Schweigen" from Georg Trakl, *Dichtungen und Briefe,* ed. Walter Killy and Hans Szklenar, ©1969;

to the Hermann Luchterhand Verlag, Darmstadt, for "Wien" (excerpt) from Albert Ehrenstein, *Gedichte und Prosa,* ed. Karl Otten, ©1961;

to Elisabeth Neumann-Viertel, Vienna, for "Die Stadt" (excerpt) from Berthold Viertel, *Die Spur,* Kurt Wolff: Leipzig, ©1913;

to the S. Fischer Verlag, Frankfurt a.M., for "An den Leser," "Der schöne strahlende Mensch" from Franz Werfel, *Gesammelte Werke,* ©1967;

to the Kösel-Verlag, Munich, for "Ein alter Tibetteppich," "Weltflucht" (excerpt), "Gebet" (excerpt), "Versöhnung" (excerpt) from Else Lasker-Schüler, *Gesammelte Werke in drei Bänden,* ed. Friedhelm Kemp, vol. 1, ©1961;

to Albert Ronsin, in behalf of the Bibliothèque Municipale, Saint-Dié, for "Café" by Iwan Goll, cited after the version in *Die Aktion,* vol. 4 (1918), rpt. Verlag Klett-Cotta, ©1961; for "Der neue Orpheus" (excerpt) from Iwan Goll, *Unter keinem Stern geboren,* ed. Klaus Schuhmann, Aufbau-Verlag: Berlin, ©1973;

I wish also to gratefully acknowledge the kind permission granted by Max K. Pechstein to reproduce for the frontispiece the woodcut by Max Pechstein from the cover of *An alle Künstler!,* Willi Simon: Berlin, ©1919.

to the Verlad der Nation, Berlin, for "Vereinigung der Räterepubliken" (excerpt) from Rudolf Leonard, *Ein Leben im Gedicht,* ©1964, cited after the version in *Expressionismus Lyrik,* ed. Martin Reso et al., Aufbau-Verlag: Berlin, ©1969;

Chronology

1909   The circle "Der Neue Club" is founded around Kurt Hiller in Berlin (March); Stefan Zweig's manifesto "Das neue Pathos" appears (September).

1910   Herwarth Walden establishes the journal *Der Sturm* in Berlin (March), and the literary evenings sponsored by his circle since 1903 become an extension of the new journal; Jakob van Hoddis composes "Weltende" (May) and Georg Heym "Ophelia" (November); "Das neopathetische Cabaret," the literary cabaret of "Der Neue Club," opens in Berlin (June); the journal *Der Brenner* is founded in Innsbruck (June); the journal *Pan* resumes publication under Expressionist sponsorship (November); Alfred Richard Meyer's poetry series "Lyrische Flugblätter" begins to clearly favor Expressionists.

1911   *Der Demokrat,* under Franz Pfemfert's editorship, publishes Hoddis's "Weltende" (January); Heinrich Mann's politico-literary manifesto "Geist und Tat" appears in *Pan* (January); Pfemfert founds the journal *Die Aktion* in Berlin (February); Carl Sternheim's comedy *Die Hose* premieres in Berlin (February); Georg Heym's volume of poetry *Der ewige Tag* appears (April); Erich Mühsam's *Kain: Zeitschrift für Menschlichkeit* begins to appear in Munich; Hiller opens his Berlin cabaret "Der Gnu" (November); Max Brod reads from Franz Werfel's poetry at the second (December) of the recital evenings launched by *Die Aktion* in March; Franz Werfel's book of poems *Der Weltfreund* appears (December); by the end of the year all members of the painters' group "Die Brücke" have moved to Berlin.

1912   *Der Brenner* begins to sponsor literary evenings (January); the first of the art exhibitions of *Der Sturm* is held (March); Gottfried Benn's *Morgue und andere Gedichte* appears (March); F. T. Marinetti visits Berlin and circulates his first Futurist manifesto (April); *Der Kondor,* the first anthology of Expressionist poetry, edited by Kurt Hiller, appears (May); Alfred Kerr, having just assumed editorship of *Pan,* initiates the journal's series of "fortgeschrittene Lyrik" (May); Carl Einstein's novel *Bebuquin oder die Dilettanten des Wunders* is serialized in *Die Aktion* (July ff.); Alfred Richard Meyer's journal *Die Bücherei Maiandros* begins publication (October); Albert Ehrenstein's novel *Tubutsch,* with drawings by Oskar Kokoschka, is published; the almanac *Der Blaue Reiter,* edited by Wassily Kandinsky and Franz Marc appears in Munich; Alfred Lichtenstein's volume of poems *Die Dämmerung* and Franz Jung's volume of short stories *Das Trottelbuch* are published.

1913   Guillaume Apollinaire and Robert Delaunay visit *Der Sturm* in Berlin, where Delaunay's work is being shown, and Apollinaire lectures there on Cubism (January); Ludwig Rubiner, Friedrich Eisenlohr, and Livingstone Hahn, frequenting Expressionist circles in Paris, compose cooperatively their *Kriminal-Sonette* (spring); Alfred Döblin's *Die Ermordung einer Butterblume und andere Erzählungen* appears (spring); Georg Trakl's *Gedichte* are published (May); "Der jüngste Tag," a series edited by Kurt Wolff in Leipzig, begins to appear (May); the journal *Das Neue Pathos* is founded (May); Heinrich Bachmair's journal *Die Neue Kunst* is launched in Munich (July) and begins sponsoring literary evenings (fall); the first issue of *Die Weissen Blätter* comes out in Leipzig (September); *Revolution,* another journal edited by the Bachmair circle in Munich, begins its short life (October); Ernst Wilhelm Lotz' poetry *Und schöne Raubtierflecken...* appears (October); *Die Weisheit der Langenweile,* a collection of Kurt Hiller's essays and critiques, appears (fall); Else Lasker-Schüler's *Hebräische Balladen* are published (fall); Ernst Blass's collection of poetry *Die Strassen komme ich entlang geweht* appears (December); Ernst Stadler's major collection of poems, *Der Aufbruch,* is published (December); Kurt Pinthus's program for a new cinema, *Das Kinobuch,* comes out at the end of the year (publication date: 1914).

1914   Ernst Blass, having moved to Heidelberg from Berlin, begins to edit his journal *Die Argonauten* (January); the journal *Neue Jugend* is launched by a group of Berlin *gymnasium* students (March); Hugo Ball, with the support of other Munich artists, is developing plans for an "expressionistisches Theater" (March); Wilhelm Herzog's journal *Das*

Forum begins to appear in Munich (April); August Stramm's first poems are published in *Der Sturm* (April ff.); Iwan Goll's long poem *Der Panama-Kanal* appears (summer); the first part of Heinrich Mann's novel *Der Untertan* appears in print (the complete novel is finally published in 1918); Ernst Rowohlt, Kurt Pinthus, Walter Hasenclever, and others meet on New Year's Eve in Weimar to voice their opposition to the First World War.

1915   Hugo Ball and his friends demonstrate against the war on the balcony of Else Hadwiger's Berlin apartment on New Year's Day; Kasimir Edschmid's short stories *Die sechs Mündungen* are published (May); the journal *Die Dachstube* (after 1918: *Das Tribunal)* is launched by *gymnasium* students in Darmstadt.

1916   *Die Weissen Blätter* begins to appear in Zurich a few weeks after it was moved there for political reasons by its editor, René Schickele (January); the "Cabaret Voltaire" opens in Zurich (February) and the only issue of *Cabaret Voltaire,* the first of several Zurich Dada journals, is published (May); *Neue Jugend* resumes publication under a largely new circle of Berlin poets (July) and begins sponsoring literary evenings (September); Walter Hasenclever's play *Der Sohn* premieres in Prague (September); and Dresden (October); Johannes R. Becher's poems *An Europa* are published (fall); Kurt Hiller's politically oriented *Ziel* yearbooks begin to appear (end of the year); Pfemfert launches three new series: "Aktions-Bücher der Aeternisten," "Die Aktions-Lyrik," "Politische Aktions-Bibliothek."

1917   Georg Kaiser's play *Die Bürger von Calais* premieres in Frankfurt (January); Kasimir Edschmid delivers his lecture on "Expressionismus in der Dichtung" (December); Pfemfert initiates his series "Der rote Hahn" and begins sponsoring art exhibitions (December).

1918   *Menschen,* a journal edited by Felix Stiemer and Heinar Schilling, an outcome of the literary gatherings of the "Gruppe 1917," begins to appear in Dresden (January); the circle around *Neue Jugend* is again reorganized and helps to launch the Berlin school of Dada in a series of recitals begun in February; Reinhard Goering's *Seeschlacht* premieres in Dresden (February); Leonhard Frank's collection of short stories *Der Mensch ist gut* appears (summer); Wolf

Przygode's journal *Die Dichtung* begins to appear in Munich (winter 1917-18), his circle of friends having sponsored regular literary evenings since the spring of 1916; *Das junge Deutschland,* a journal devoted primarily to Expressionist theater, is launched (fall); the first production of the troupe "Sturm-Bühne," August Stramm's *Sancta Susanna,* premieres in Berlin under Lothar Schreyer's direction (October), and soon thereafter the troupe moves to Hamburg; the revolutionary organization of artists "Die Novembergruppe" is founded on the heels of the German November Revolution; Karl Otten's poems *Die Thronerhebung des Herzens* appear.

1919   The only issue of *"Jedermann sein eigner Fussball"* appears, the first of several Berlin Dada journals (February); *Kameraden der Menschheit,* an anthology of Expressionist revolutionary poems edited by Ludwig Rubiner, is published (spring); the theater group "Die Tribüne" begins sponsoring productions of Expressionist plays in Berlin, including Ernst Toller's *Die Wandlung* (September); *An alle Künstler!,* a collection of art and literature inspired by the Revolution, appears; the series "Sturm-Bücher" is launched; Kasimir Edschmid initiates a series of manifestoes, "Tribüne der Kunst und Zeit"; Paul Steegemann begins to issue volumes in the series "Die Silbergäule" in Hannover; the poetry anthology *Menschheitsdämmerung,* edited by Kurt Pinthus, appears at the end of the year (dated 1920).

1920   Berlin Dada breaks up after the last group exhibition (June); *Verkündigung,* an anthology of Expressionist poetry, appears and its editor, Rudolf Kayser, introduces a note of gloom and despair in the foreword which is totally new to Expressionism; most Expressionist journals have ceased publication by the end of the year; the numbers of necrologies of the movement in the press increases; the release of *Das Cabinett des Dr. Caligari* gives Expressionism a solid foothold in the cinema (after tenuous beginnings before the war under Kurt Pinthus and Paul Wegener (February).

1924   Of the important journals of the Expressionist movement, only three *(Der Sturm, Der Brenner, Die Aktion)* survive this year; no new Expressionist journals have been founded since 1920; there are few signs of Expressionist group efforts or activities after this year.

CHAPTER 1

Introduction

T HE main subject of this study is Expressionist poetry, but its
scope will be considerably broader. Considering the unsettled
state of scholarship on the question of Expressionism as a period
concept, the poetry cannot really be reassessed without reassessing
the whole movement as well. The problem of defining Expression-
ism has rarely been faced head on since Richard Brinkmann called
for a precise definition in a noted 1959-60 review of research. In the
last two decades, as the flow of studies of Expressionism from the
presses of Europe and America has steadily swelled, the term has
most often been used uncritically, as a convenient period tag, with
the problem of definition being left to the future. But this kind of
evasion is no longer necessary; our purview of the movement is
much more profound today. The many reprints of Expressionist
publications long out of print (in particular the vast number of
journals and volumes in series sponsored by Expressionist circles),
the appearance of a whole corpus of letters, diaries, and remin-
iscences by the Expressionists themselves and the rapid growth of
the accessible collection of Expressionist manuscripts and books in
the Deutsches Literaturarchiv of the Schiller-National museum,
Marbach a.N. — all of this has provided us with sufficient insight
into the intimate workings of Expressionism as a literary movement
to yield a more comprehensive perspective on it.

The basic weakness in previous approaches to this subject was
narrowness. They concentrated largely on stylistic and thematic
tendencies alone, i. e., on purely literary features; they ignored the
conditioning cultural context from which the literature emanated
and in which it found most of its themes and the impetus for its
stylistic devices. No literature is created in a vacuum, of course,
and no literary movement which lasts for over a decade could possi-
bly resist the demands for change made on it by the simple passage
of time. With Expressionism in particular, the general political, so-

cial, economic, historical, as well as literary background is of central importance. This fact is true, if for no other reason than merely because Expressionism was much more than just an artistic revolution: the reach of its activities extended into most areas of human intellectual endeavor, its adherents participating in agitation for, and implementation of, change in politics, economics, social structures, publishing, music, philosophy, psychology, film, theater, architecture, painting, and literature. Thus, when we discuss Expressionism we cannot talk solely of literary matters, especially if we wish to understand it for what it was — a coherent movement in the fullest sense of the term.

The concept of a literary movement is indispensable to the approach to Expressionist poetry in the present study. However, since literary history has failed to provide a clear understanding of the concept (it is glossed, for example, in very few of the standard handbooks to literature and nowhere substantively), I will have to venture my own definition before I can proceed any further.[1]

The Random House Dictionary of the English Language provides us with a solid starting point. It describes a "movement" (in both a political and artistic sense) as "a diffusely organized or heterogeneous group of people or organizations tending toward or favoring a generalized goal."[2] I will treat Expressionism therefore as a heterogeneous complex of loosely organized and affiliated, yet tangibly identifiable groups of artists, who were working cooperatively toward common goals, employing thereby common means (e.g., styles and themes) and publicizing their positions artistically or programmatically in/on common literary or politico-literary tribunes. It has been conclusively established that Expressionism constituted such a development on the level of literary life: i.e., as far as group activities are concerned — the formation of circles that met on a fairly regular basis, the organization of public events (recitals, balls, etc.), the coediting of journals, sponsoring a common program, etc.[3] The present study will attempt to show that this can also be said of the literature.

If, indeed, the literature I am about to discuss was the product of a movement, then that fact alone justifies giving it a special name. But the reader will ask: Why "Expressionism"? There are several reasons why this label is still the most appropriate, in spite of the many challenges to it.

First of all, unlike similar period tags (e.g., "Baroque," "Biedermeier"), "Expressionism" was not introduced in the current sense by art or literary critics not associated with, or sympathetic to, the work it now identifies. The first appearance of the term in the modern sense occurred in 1911 — if we exclude as hearsay an anecdote told by Theodor Däubler, according to which Paul Cassirer (a contemporary sponsor of Expressionist painters and writers) was the first to use the term in Germany in 1910 to describe a canvas by Max Pechstein.[4] As Arnim Arnold reports, the first documented use of the term occurred in the preface to a catalogue for the twenty-second exhibition of the Berlin Secession, held in the spring and summer of 1911. It was applied to the work of the French "Expressionists," i.e., the Fauvists and Cubists (Georges Braque, André Derain, Pablo Picasso, Maurice de Vlaminck, et al.).[5] By the beginning of the next year, Walter Serner, a member of the Expressionist camp, was using the term in the journal *Die Aktion (Action)* in a review of German painters participating in a show sponsored by the progressive Berlin artists' association called the New Secession. Most of the artists Serner named would still be considered representative of the movement: Wassily Kandinsky, Ernst Ludwig Kirchner, Artur Segal, Karl Schmidt-Rottluff, Max Pechstein, Georg Tappert, Heinrich Richter-Berlin, Emil Nolde, and others.[6]

Paul Raabe has established 1911 as the year of the first application of the term to German literature. This took place in an article written for the literary supplement to the *Heidelberger Zeitung* by Kurt Hiller, who was then rapidly becoming a leading spokesman of the movement. The article is a survey of the recent developments in the new Berlin literary avant-garde (Ferdinand Hardekopf, Ernst Blass, Georg Heym, Ludwig Rubiner, Erich Unger, et al.), among which Hiller at one point includes himself when he declares: "Those aesthetes, who only know how to react, who are only wax plates for impressions and machines for recording the minute details of descriptions...seem inferior to us. We are Expressionists. We are once more concerned with the contents, the intent, the ethos."[7] Others followed Hiller's lead in the ensuing years; and by no later than 1914, when we find the term being used by several writers associated with its literary manifestations (Iwan Goll, Käthe Brodnitz, Hugo Ball, Eduard Korrodi, Arthur Kronfeld, Friedrich Markus Huebner, Ernst Stadler), it had clearly and self-consciously been ensconced inside the thinking of the movement.[8] During the war it was popularized in the broader public by numerous friends and foes of the movement, including Otto Flake, René Schickele,

Kasimir Edschmid, Gerhard Heine, Franz Herwig, Herwarth Walden, Theodor Däubler, Friedrich Koffka, Karl Otten, Paul Hatvani, and others.[9] Finally, by 1918 it was appearing widely as the official slogan of journals associated with the movement.

The term not only enjoyed wide popularity during the Expressionist era, it has also become an indispensable part of literary history. Since the publication of the first major study of the literature in 1925, Albert Soergel's *Dichtung und Dichter der Zeit: Im Banne des Expressionismus,* literary historians have consistently demonstrated their reluctance to abandon the term.

Lastly, the term continues — again, in spite of all the disputes about its meaning — to denote something quite specific for us as readers. We know rather precisely which authors are usually subsumed under it, even if we do not always know exactly why.

In view of all these facts, we will have to acknowledge that "Expressionism" is not only an appropriate label for the German artistic avant-garde from about 1910-1924, but also a term that is decidedly here to stay. Yet still another question is often raised by critics: Which authors and which works of this literature deserve our attention?

I have already suggested how great was the scope of interests and activities of the Expressionists. The number of those involved were equally great. Some 200 or more writers were clearly and substantially identified with the movement's many activities. On this basis alone diversity must be expected to be an inherent factor in Expressionist literature. Moreover, if we wish to assess the literature as part and product of the movement, i.e., to understand Expressionism rather than just some Expressionists, then we must be open to the work of all its representatives, not only to that of the "best." I will therefore have to be somewhat uncritical in my selection of representative poems, for some of the best examples of the aims of Expressionism are not always the best of its accomplishments. Thus the reader will find highly regarded poets, such as Georg Trakl, Gottfried Benn, Georg Heym, Ernst Stadler, and Else Lasker-Schüler, whose work often transcends its role in Expressionism, discussed side by side with poets who are rarely of more than historical interest.

In addition, we will have to be open to all kinds of writing, at least as background to the poetry. The theoretical writings of Expressionism are especially crucial here. Expressionism was a true movement, and it is of the nature of a movement that it will want to explain, justify, and promote itself. Contrary to a not uncommon critical opinion, the programmatic writings of Expressionism neither preceded nor postdated the literature; rather, they generally accompanied it. A cursory look at the journals of the movement, in which the program is mixed with the imaginative literature, not relegated to a separate section, demonstrates this. It was no different in the poet's studio: his programmatic writing was penned along with — not clearly before or after — his poems; each conditioned and shaped the other. The poems as a body thus come out of an environment highly charged with self-conscious aesthetic, political, economic, or social theorizing. To cite some examples; Jakob van Hoddis composed his famous doomsday poem "Weltende" ("World's End," 1910) during the time he was regularly attending sessions of an Expressionist circle, in which the central theme of both philosophical discussion and public manifesto was the coming "apocalypse." In December, 1912 Ernst Blass published a collection of urban-based poetry, composed while he was a member of the circle just mentioned. Its leader, Hiller, had been calling specifically for such poetry for more than a year. Blass also assumed the same theoretical position as his close friend Hiller in his "Preface" (not "afterword"!) to the poems. Finally, Rudolf Kurtz formulated the program with which the first issue of the journal *Der Sturm (The Storm)* opened on March 3, 1910; and a whole body of literature, broadly matching the principles outlined by Kurtz, appeared in the journal's pages in the years that followed. In fact, the volume of Expressionist theoretical writings suggests their importance for the Expressionists themselves.[10] Much of Expressionist poetry — Benn's verse provides some of the best examples in this context — is all too self-consciously programmatic itself to permit us to make any firm assertions about the chronological primacy of poetry over against theory. But beyond any such proofs as to the nature of the relationship between these two literary forms, any categorical statements on this question are naive, for there are no absolutes concerning the creative process; its methods and manners are infinitely variable, virtually as diverse as the numbers of its practitioners. We must therefore use all the information and material at our disposal in an effort to understand each of its manifestations.

It would clearly obviate continuing this study beyond the Introduction, if I were to state in detail at this stage what "Expressionism," or exactly what an "Expressionist," is; that, after all, is what this book is all about. It might be helpful to the reader, however, if I anticipate, as a way of outlining the study, some of the very general modes of literary and politico-literary behavior common to the Expressionists, which will be detailed and illustrated in the pages that follow.

As Chapter 2 suggests, the broad historical context of Expressionism is a crucial factor in determining the nature of the poetry of the movement. Chapter 3 begins the delineation of this context, outlining the common cultural background from which the Expressionists came. With few exceptions, they were all born between about 1875 and 1895. They came of age in, were conditioned by, and responded to, the same political, economic, social, and philosophical situation: the crisis-ridden era of German imperialist and industrial expansion under William II. Chapter 4 describes the specific ways in which this common background found expression in their lives and work. This chapter establishes the politico-literary unity of Expressionism, on which is based the discussion in the subsequent chapters of its more strictly literary cohesiveness. In their poetry, the Expressionists demonstrated a common preoccupation with their urban surroundings, its sounds, sights, and issues. They assumed together responsibility for the future of man, in an age which seemed to them to neglect his deepest needs in favor rebellious defiance of what they considered to be the arbitrary, imaginary, and myopic version of reality according to established perception; and they joined forces in an attempt to reunify a world divided by their contemporaries. They participated together in a highly active artistic community as an alternative to the stultifying lifestyle of their society. Finally, they shared in a common development: first searching for answers in the uncharted regions of philosophical inquiry and artistic expression (1910-14), then being overwhelmed by the battlefields of war on which most of them fought (1914-18) and finally attempting to fight for solutions to the ills of their age through political revolution in the streets of their own cities (1918 ff.). As all of their common experiences and interests found creative expression, the related styles (Chapter 5) and themes (Chapter 6) of their work united the Expressionists artistically.

CHAPTER 2

Prologue: The Literary Scene
Around 1910

IN 1896, the young Hugo von Hofmannsthal (1874-1929) gave a lecture entitled "Poetry and Life" that has since come to be considered one of the major statements of Impressionist philosophy. Hofmannsthal said:

> The material of poetry is its words.... The words are everything.... There is no direct path from poetry into life, from life into poetry. The word as bearer of a content drawn from life and its dreamlike counterpart, which can stand in a poem, are completely foreign to one another. No external law bans from poetry any reasoning about, any fault-finding with life, any direct reference to life and any direct imitation of life; rather the simple impossibility of it does: such weighty things as those can no more live in poetry than cows in tree-tops.[1]

In 1915, Kurt Pinthus (1886-1975) published a major critical and theoretical statement on the literature that had followed Hofmannsthal's by some twenty years. He wrote of the "new poetry" of Expressionism:

> The new art, which...is not concerned with appearances and ornamentation but with essences, the heart and the core of things, which is against any reality imposed from without and is fighting for a more intensive, more noble — let us dare say: better existence, is after all...a political poetry....[2]

Here are two philosophies expressed by young poets scarcely one generation apart in time, but diametrically opposed in point of view. For the first, poetry is clearly "art for art's sake": it is divorced from specific purpose and from real life. In art seen from this perspective, the poet does not take a stand on issues or concerns in the world created by human governments and human industry. Its subject matter is found strictly in the poetic fancy of its creator. For the second theorist, poetry is a "littérature engagée," as committed as politics is to specific goals and vital issues.[3] Art, for Pinthus, seizes hold of life, wrings from it the pains and joys it dispenses upon man and tries to evaluate and reshape it.

The mere juxtaposition of those two theoretical statements draws attention to a significant quality of Expressionism. In many important ways it was a conscious, radical break with literary and philosophical traditions of the past, especially the immediate past represented by Hofmannsthal's generation. Thus, it is useful to have some notion of what preceded Expressionism in order to clearly understand and appreciate the achievements of its poetry. I cannot provide the reader with a history of German poetry, but it will serve our purpose well enough if I begin this study by simply comparing two representative poems of the opposing traditions at the time the Expressionist movement was launched (ca. 1910). The first of these poems represents the established style; it is by Stefan George (1868-1933), alongside Hofmannsthal a leading poet of the turn of the century. The second poem signals the break with the past; it is a poem which, in 1911, quickly helped to establish the young Prague poet Franz Werfel (1890-1945) as a major voice in Expressionism:

Komm in den totgesagten park und schau. . .(1897)

Komm in den totgesagten park und schau:
Der schimmer ferner lächelnder gestade·
Der reinen wolken unverhofftes blau
Erhellt die weiher und die bunten pfade.

Dort nimm das tiefe gelb· das weiche grau
Von birken und von buchs· der wind ist lau·
Die späten rosen welkten noch nicht ganz·
Erlese küsse sie und flicht den kranz.

Vergiss auch diese letzten astern nicht·
Den purpur um die ranken wilder reben
Und auch was übrig blieb von grünem leben
Verwinde leicht im herbstlichen gesicht.[4]

Come into the Park They Think is Dead . . .

Come into the park they think is dead· behold:
The shimmer of the distant smiling shores·
The unexpected blue of pristine clouds
Illumes the ponds and brightly colored paths.

There take the yellow bright· the gently gray
Of boxwood and of birch· the wind is soft·
The roses blossomed late have not yet withered·
Select and kiss them· weave the wreath.

Forget not too these final asters·
The purple round the tendrils of wild vines
And what'er else is left of verdurous life
Then gently intertwine in autumn's vision.

An den Leser (1911)

Mein einziger Wunsch ist, dir, o Mensch verwandt zu sein!
Bist du Neger, Akrobat, oder ruhst du noch in tiefer Mutterhut,
Klingt dein Mädchenlied über den Hof, lenkst du dein Floss im
    Abendschein,
Bist du Soldat, oder Aviatiker voll Ausdauer und Mut.

Trugst du als Kind auch ein Gewehr in grüner Armschlinge?
Wenn es losging, entflog ein angebundener Stöpsel dem Lauf.
Mein Mensch, wenn ich Erinnerung singe,
Sei nicht hart, und löse dich mit mir in Tränen auf!

Denn ich habe alle Schicksale durchgemacht. Ich weiss
Das Gefühl von einsamen Harfenistinnen in Kurkapellen,
Das Gefühl von schüchternen Gouvernanten im fremden Familien-
    kreis,
Das Gefühl von Debutanten, die sich zitternd vor den Souffleur-
    kasten stellen.

Ich lebte im Walde, hatte ein Bahnhofsamt,
Sass gebeugt über Kassabücher, und bediente ungeduliğe Gäste.
Als Heizer stand ich vor Kesseln, das Antlitz grell überflammt,
Und als Kuli ass ich Abfall und Küchenreste.

So gehöre ich dir und Allen!
Wolle mir, bitte, nicht widerstehn!
O, könnte es einmal geschehn,
Dass wir uns, Bruder, in die Arme fallen![5]

To the Reader

My only wish, O fellow man, is to be your brother!
Be you negro, or acrobat or nestled still in mother's wing,
Whether your maiden song rings across the yard, or you're
    steering your raft in evening's glow,
Be you soldier or aviator full of courage and endurance.

Did you also carry a rifle in green arm sling as a child?
When it went off, a cork on a string flew out of the barrel.
My fellow man, when I sing of memories,
Be not hard, but dissolve with me in tears!

For I have suffered all fates. I know
The feelings of lonely harpists in health spa bands,
The feelings of shy governesses in strange family circles,
The feelings of debutants, who stand trembling before the
    prompter's box.

I lived in the forest, was a railroad employee,
Sat poring over cash-books and served impatient guests.
I stood before boilers as a stoker, my face flaming hot,
And as a coolie ate garbage and kitchen leftovers.

Thus I belong to you and all!
Please try not to resist me!
Oh, if only one day it could be,
My brother, that we'd embrace each other.

The dominant tone of the George poem is extremely lyrical, one of tranquillity and peace. This is conditioned as much by the regularity of the form (rhymed iambic pentameter) as by the frivolousness and simplicity of the contents (the description of the beauty of a park in autumn). The poem by Werfel, on the other hand, is excited and concerned. This tone is also supported by both the form (the use of the rhetorical meter of prose, i.e., free verse and the liberal use of the exclamation point) and the theme (the poet's exuberant wish to establish a close relationship with his fellow man). George's attitude is decidedly retiring, elitist, aristocratic. He finds fulfillment in a withdrawal from human society into nature. Even his language suggests exclusiveness, reservedness: it is the traditional diction of poetry, whose esoteric dignity is further enhanced by the poet's eschewal of common practices in orthography (no use of the traditional capitalization of German nouns) and punctuation.

Werfel, very much like his mentor Walt Whitman,[6] is clearly trying to remove all the barriers between poet and audience that George so carefully constructs. He is eclectic in vision and style; he wants to share in everyman's experience, from the lowest to the highest, and is therefore not afraid to talk of pedestrian things ("popguns," "aviators," "health spa bands," "cash-books," "coolies") in an essentially pedestrian language (an almost workaday prose). For George, "beauty" is given by tradition; for Werfel it is clearly a relative concept: it can be found everywhere, even in the modern civilized world. The poet's attitude toward the reader in the two poems is also significantly different, though both address him directly. For George this fact seems either superfluous or peripheral: the imaginary reader performs merely a traditional and perfunctory task, providing the poet with a convenient means for creating his scenery. Werfel's address, however, is characterized by a tone of admonishment and urgency; it is strongly rhetorical. The poet is trying to convince, to move the reader to share in a common feeling and experience. George is clearly as content with the reader's surface emotions as he is with his own surface impressions of life. There is — to cite an Expressionist complaint against his poetry — none of the chaos of life in his limited vision. Werfel, by contrast, wants to penetrate much more deeply, to the reader's heart and to the core of life. Finally, one last difference is worth stressing in the context of Expressionism. George's world is curiously (conspicuously) unpeopled and nature-oriented (even though nature in this instance is the artificial sort represented by a park); we have the feeling that he is writing for the solitary reader. This quality is not untypical of Impressionism, which largely responds in a passive way to the world. Werfel's perspective, on the other hand, is distinctly anthropocentric. He seems to want to address the masses: like all the Expressionists, Werfel is concerned with human society, with the world created by people for people.

It should be clear by now how the theoretical positions of Hofmannsthal and Pinthus are reflected in the poetry of the eras they represent. Their positions are quite different, but not surprisingly so. They are simply conditioned ultimately by very different historical situations. The Expressionists in particular were self-consciously aware of this fact. For example, the painter Wassily Kandinsky states at the outset of his now famous theoretical work, *Über das Geistige in der Kunst (Concerning the Spiritual in Art,* 1911): "Every work of art is the child of its age and...each period

of culture produces an art of its own which can never be re-
peated."[7] This fact was often to have tragic implications for the
Expressionists, as the novelist Kasimir Edschmid stressed in a 1918
manifesto when he declared that he and his fellow Expressionists
had been "placed more fiercely at the mercy of the times, thus were
more fiercely their master, more inextricably caught up in an age
than any poets ever were, devoted to it in fatal measure."[8] George's
work is born of a world still fairly quiet, stable, secure, and self-con-
fident; he is therefore a relatively untroubled artist. Werfel's art
emanates from a world virtually out of joint, a world deeply un-
settled by social upheaval and sorely rocked by a whole series of
major political and philosophical crises. These facts help to explain
the urgency and concern in his poetic voice.

As we begin to surmise, then, the real world of tangible exper-
iences and basic concerns is quite visibly the conditioning frame-
work of Expressionism. Werfel's poem patently illustrates the
profound degree to which the Expressionists were not only en-
veloped by, but also deeply and directly concerned with, their con-
temporary world. This concern extended well beyond mere literary
or aesthetic matters to embrace most important issues of the day.
We will, therefore, have to take at least a brief look at the general
historical background of Expressionism before we can properly
consider its poetry in further detail.

CHAPTER 3

Cultural Framework

DISCONTENT, unrest, excited discussion and debate, intense activity, agitation for change, dedication to new ideals, revolution — such were the broad features of the Expressionist movement in the course of its development. But seen in historical perspective, they are scarcely unexpected features. The times themselves — from the end of the nineteenth century to the beginning of the 1930's — were of a similar nature. These were years of tremendous disturbance and change in most areas of human activity: in politics, society, economics, philosophy, art, etc. Such was, of course, not only the state of things in Germany, but throughout most of Europe as well. One historian, in a study which concentrates on the social development in this period, has spoken of an "upheaval" in Europe.[1]

I   Social and Economic Developments

In Germany the upheaval had its source socio-economically in four major developments which took place over a very short span of time but had profound effects on German society: a rapid increase in population, the second phase of industrialization, widescale urbanization, and far-reaching transformations in class structure.[2] Conditioned by several decades without major military conflict, a steady rise in the standard of living and improvements in medical care, the German population almost doubled between the middle of the nineteenth century and the outbreak of the First World War. This development strained to the limits both the economic structure and the habitable space of the country. The healthy growth of industrialization in its first phase in Europe (approximately 1800-70) had been severely inhibited in Germany by the effects of Napoleon's conquest and the lack of national unity.

But the second phase (approximately 1870-1914) — encouraged by German unification, French reparation payments after the Franco-Prussian War (1870–71), and the economic policies of Bismarck — transformed Germany in a few decades from an agrarian land into a leading industrial power. The population increase and spread of industrialization led to the urbanization of Germany. The inability of agriculture to absorb any more workers, a change in the traditional labor structure on the farms and a series of agricultural crises drove increasing numbers of farm laborers and their families into the cities in search of factory work. In 1871 two-thirds of the population still lived in the country, while by 1914 that percentage had been cut in half; and whereas only five percent of the population lived in large cities in 1877, by 1910 the figure had increased more than four-fold. Cities with over 100,000 inhabitants virtually exploded in numbers at the turn of the century: in 1800 there were merely two such cities in all of Germany; by 1850 the number had only doubled; but two decades later the increases began to become dramatic: 1871: eight; 1880: fourteen; 1890: twenty-six; 1900: thirty-three; and 1910: forty-eight (!). The population density also intensified dramatically, in spite of new territories acquired and massive emigration by Germans abroad.

It is only to be expected that, under the pressure of all these developments, the old class structure would crumble and give way to a new one. The only new class actually to appear in this period was that of the factory workers: under the influence of the labor unions between 1871 and 1914, they soon developed into a self-conscious, class-conscious mass. The old class of the Junkers (the landed aristocracy) generally combined forces and interests with the peasant farmers in opposition to the industrialists. And, finally, by 1914, one could no longer speak of the burghers as a social class or rank: the old middle class had split up by this time into several separate groups, including most prominently the big industrialists, the white collar workers, and the professionals with extensive education ("Bildungsbürgertum").

II   *Science and Technology*

The developments described above seriously undermined the socio-economic foundations of the old order. And the challenges to it on other levels were equally formidable. The sciences altered the appearance of reality with numerous technological advances, as the spread of earlier developments quickened in pace now, too. Most of these advances had an overwhelming impact on the daily lives of the average citizen. The spread of the railroad to all important cities was completed in this era, and electricity found ever increasing uses, especially in lighting and in powering vehicles and telephones. A new medium was added to communication: the motion picture (first demonstrated publicly in a Berlin theater in 1895) could already count its fans in the millions by the beginning of the Expressionist era. A new dimension was given to human experience when the first successful experiments in motorized flight were carried out with dirigibles (1900 ff.) and airplanes (1903 ff.). The electric streetcar, the automobile (there were already 55,000 automobiles on German streets by 1914), the motorcycle and the bicycle — combined with all the developments discussed earlier — radically changed the face of German cities. Formerly, they had been densely populated and busy, yet still relatively quiet, places, in which most transportation was by friendly and slow-moving horse-drawn carriages and trams. Now they became bustling, overcrowded, noisy, and problem-ridden, their streets often threatening or dangerous to pedestrians. Life was lived in them at the hectic pace of the work on the factory assembly lines that fed them with people and goods. The city-dweller's eye was daily bombarded on the streets and in the shops with an overwhelming variety of multi-colored impressions. The city had become a dynamic and imposing place to live in and its influence insistent on the lives of its inhabitants.

III *Philosophy*

Theoreticians of the exact sciences, such as Albert Einstein and Max Planck, were beginning to question the established theoretical perspectives on the natural world. But the most effective formulation of the intellectual challenge to the old order came from the pen of a philosopher whose following throughout this era was literally cultic: Friedrich Nietzsche (1844–1900).[3]

Although he died in 1900, Nietzsche has often been called the prophet of the twentieth century because he foresaw so well the crisis of faith that was to haunt our age. His philosophy, however, has an essentially affirmative core. As one of his leading interpreters has put it, Nietzsche's thought is an attempt to "strengthen the heritage of the Enlightenment with a more profound understanding of the irrational."[4] What Nietzsche thus achieved in such provocative and widely read works as *The Birth of Tragedy* (1872), *Thus Spoke Zarathustra* (1883-85), *Beyond Good and Evil* (1886), and *The Antichrist* (1895) is a redefinition of man's essence which finally accommodated the side of human character so long suppressed in Western philosophy.[5] Descartes's thesis that man creates his essence through cognition *("cogito, ergo sum")* is challenged by Nietzsche's claim that the basis of being is willing: life is ruled not by a rational process which imitates the mind of God, but by a self-determined drive, the will to power, that blindly desires to assert and fulfill itself. In Nietzsche's view, reason, traditionally placed at the core of human nature, is but the ultimate manifestation of the will to power.

Man therefore stands alone on earth with his will to power. He can expect no help from the supernatural in establishing the meaning of life, for "God is dead": he was the invention of the theologians, and ceased to live once faith had died.[5] There are thus no absolutes; knowledge and truth are relative. Nothing is eternal, except for the unending recurrence throughout time of all things in earthly existence. Nietzsche rejects the Christian doctrine of an afterlife, because it favors death at the expense of life: for him, the sole good is life. Yet he also rejects the materialism of the middle class, since it diverts attention from the true seat of good by seeking it in the external world rather than within the self. He argues for a transvaluation of the Christian concepts of virtue, pity, justice, since they suppress man's real nature and thereby enslave all men, inhibiting the strong and pacifying the weak. And traditional virtues pervert both reason (into rigid logic) and passion (into unfulfilling lust).

Nietzsche postulates a new morality based on his conception of human essence. Its code reads: beyond conventional notions of good and evil lies the real good — being true to one's self; beyond established authority lies the only path to truth — following the lead of the self. Evil is now whatever inhibits the will to power; good is whatever enhances it. The old morality is embodied in the old man, in Zarathustra's "last man." The new morality is born in the new man: he is an intellectually unfettered, a self-sufficient and self-consistent man, whom Zarathustra hails as the "overman."

In the year of Nietzsche's death, a book appeared which provided his correction of Descartes with surprising scientific support. It is another seminal work of the period, by another thinker sometimes referred to as a path-finder of our century: Sigmund Freud's

The Interpretation of Dreams.[6] Without any apparent dependence on Nietzsche, Freud arrived in this study at conclusions concerning human nature which are astonishingly close to those of the philosopher.

Freud postulated in preliminary form (to be worked out in more detail in later studies) two levels of mental activity in the human psyche: the primary and the secondary processes. The first of these processes is centered in the unconscious and dominated by the pleasure principle or irrational wishing. This is the sphere of activity of what Freud later called the "id," a force generated solely by intellectual cathexes (concentrated psychic energy) seeking discharge. It is therefore a force which "knows no values, no good and evil, no morality."[7] The secondary process is, as Freud would later put it, the sphere of activity of the "superego," a force which is now unconscious, now preconscious and, in the extreme, conscious and perceptual-conscious. It is this process that enforces the standards and demands of the external world. Finally, caught between what Freud calls the "three tyrants" of the external world, the id, and the superego, there is the beleaguered "ego," which attempts to mediate between the other forces in the psyche and to synthesize them all into a unified personality.

The central generating force in the psyche in Freud's system is the irrational wish. Freud concluded that all thinking is little more than a detour around, and a frustration of, this central force. Even the perceptual process, the exploration of reality, is motivated by the pleasure principle. Freud summarizes this point near the end of his study of dreams: "Thinking is indeed nothing but a substitute for the hallucinatory wish; and if the dream is called a wish-fulfillment, this becomes something self-evident, since nothing but a wish can impel our psychic apparatus to activity."[8]

IV   *Politics*

Most of the years between 1871 and mid-1914 were years of great prosperity and security for a significant number of Germans, whose country was rising to the position of leading industrial power in Europe, second in the world only to the United States.[9] In spite of severe economic slumps in the 1870's and 1880's, the general economic trend was strongly upward. The gross national product increased by an astonishing 240 percent and the per capita income by over 40 percent. Even the salaries of the factory workers rose steadily at a noticeable pace. The average number of working hours per day fell from twelve to nine-and-one-half. The first social legislation was introduced (1883 ff.); it provided for national old age retirement, accident and health insurance, designated Sunday as a day of rest from labor, and strictly limited the working hours of women and children. Mass production in the factories made luxuries more readily available to a much larger segment of the population. And German society began to offer its masses an ever greater variety of recreation and entertainment (theaters, movie houses, sports, parks, travel, etc.). The rate of German emigration plunged sharply after its historic high in the 1880's. The standard of living was clearly on the rise at home; and people were, on the whole, more content.

All these factors, in conjunction with the long absence (1871-14) of any major military confrontation in Europe, gave most Germans a sense of security. The prosperity was certainly real for most observers. But many sensitive minds felt that the sense of security was deceptive. For these were, in fact, politically contradictory years. As one historian has written: "The prevailing mood was a blend of *hubris,* fear and frustration."[10] Bethmann Hollweg, Chancellor from 1909 to 1917, even detected an atmosphere of oppression and dissatisfaction in German political life on the eve of the war.[11] This mood stemmed primarily from the repeated political crises that beset Germany in the decade and a half before the First World War. They were crises that never climaxed, but which were nonetheless constant reminders of the instability of a regime threatened both from within and without its borders by forces of discontent.

A leading role in fostering this prevailing mood was played by Kaiser William II (1859–1941), who acceded to the throne in 1888, following the death of his father, Frederick III. The Second Empire was a constitutional monarchy, in which political power was divided among the Kaiser, the Chancelor, and the parliament. One of the major sources of trouble in the Wilhelminian era was the uncertainty as to where exactly the base of power resided in the government.[12] In 1870, Chancellor Otto von Bismarck had cemented the Empire together out of many disparate and otherwise incompatible entities. Thereafter, he had succeeded in holding the nation together largely by dint of his strong and unswerving personality. But he was dismissed by the young William II in 1890, in what was basically a dispute over authority in the government. This turned out to be the most important political act of William II's entire reign. For more than ever before, the new empire needed a personality like Bismarck's at its helm in order to get through the crises in the years ahead. William II unfortunately did not have such a personality.

The Empire's new ruler had many engaging qualities: he was youthful, intelligent, energetic. He was full of interest and enthusiasm for new things and new ideas. His eloquence in conversation and gregarious nature were said to have had a fascinating effect on his audiences. Yet, all of these qualities had their converse sides as well. His interests probably ranged too wide: he has often been criticized for being a dilettante. He was opinionated, and the superficiality of his knowledge often did more harm than good to the country. His judgments were frequently impulsive and erratic, and his behavior was sometimes offensive or tactless. Not infrequently his exuberance degenerated into simple brashness, his glibness into bombast. The wide-spread dissatisfaction with his regime is exemplified, if not epitomized, by the notorious *"Daily Telegraph* Affair.'' This scandal resulted from a private interview which William II gave to a retired British officer. In a well-meant attempt to improve the poor relations between Germany and England, he indiscreetly disclosed to the officer diplomatic secrets of the most delicate nature and of potential embarrassment to both England and Germany. Astonishingly enough, with the Kaiser's permission, a transcript of the interview was published in the London newspaper, *The Daily Telegraph,* on Oct. 28, 1908. It launched a storm of protest in German political circles, brought to the surface much of the bitter frustration over William II's reign long harbored by even his closest associates, and precipitated an actual crisis in parliament.

The Kaiser also played no small part in bringing about the other, more serious crises and conflicts that endangered Germany's position in world politics. This was the age of imperialism; and in this world obsessed with power, Germany, like the other major industrial states, was vying for its "place in the sun."[13] But Germany was at a fateful disadvantage in the competition, for she was eventually forced into a position of political isolation between the members of the Triple Entente (France, England, and Russia). This fact alone robbed Germany of much of her self-confidence. Her only solid ally throughout the era was Austria; but Austria's allegiance proved to be more a burden than an asset. Germany's insistence on significant enlargements in the naval fleet (especially after 1904) crippled from the start her repeated attempts at rapprochement with the British. Whenever she became embroiled in conflicts abroad, she inevitably exacerbated her already troubled relations with the other powers. Her involvement in Southern Africa (1895-1900), which at an early stage even involved support of the anti-British Boers, put her at odds with England. Intervention in China in 1898 and 1900, which included the seizure of the port of Kiao-Chow and suppression of the Boxer uprising, placed her in direct competition with all three members of the Entente. Her sponsorship of the Bagdad Railway Project (1898 ff.) threatened Russian interests in the Near East, while her posture in disputes over Morocco (1905-06, 1911) antagonized the French. Most fateful was Germany's support of the Austrian position in the Balkan crises (1908, 1912-13), the immediate prologue to World War I. All of these conflicts not only conditioned her relations with the other colonial powers, they also drew attention to the growing threats from unrest among the masses in the suppressed nations. —Meanwhile, trouble was brewing at home, too, for Germany's own masses were also becoming restless.

The widening gulf between the haves and the have-nots, and the attendant growth of socialism, is one of the most crucial facts in German history after 1871. Ideologically, the gulf was probably wider in this period than at any other time. The German workers had begun to develop their own dynamics as a class through self-conscious awareness of their role as both product and creator of industrial society.[14] They now demanded, with growing insistence, a larger share of the country's wealth and more equitable representation in the government. The significance of their challenge to the ruling classes is witnessed by the massive growth of support for the union movement and the Social Democratic Party, especially between 1900 and 1912 (by which time over one-third of the voters were enrolled within the party's ranks). The history of the Wilhelminian era on this level is the story of a new industrial state trying vainly to reconcile its new class of malcontent workers with the reactionary forces of tradition and vested interests.

V   *The Dominant Values*

Throughout these years of turmoil and change, the people with position and power were struggling desperately to maintain the status quo. They attempted to do this morally by enforcing a set of values which represented an odd heterogeneous fusion of traditional upper-class and middle-class principles with the new standards of the capitalist bourgeoisie.

The upper class contributed its reactionary outlook to this ethical gallimaufry: an emphasis on militarism, strict observance of class barriers and the principle of deference to authority. The soldier, identified with principles of honor and a regimented lifestyle, became the ideal man. The Kaiser helped to reinforce this notion by often appearing publicly in military dress and displaying an unusually strong interest in military and naval affairs. The soldier was a symbol of the hierarchy of authority which every citizen was expected to obey: it began with the emperor and reached down through the military, the police, the schools, and ended in the family, where it was embodied first and most tangibly in the head of the family. The old middle class contributed its traditional values of self-restraint, diligence, and order. All things were done for the sake, and in the name, of economic success: hard work, proper education, and pedantic regularity in private and professional life. Pleasure was something to be taken only in moderate doses. Idiosyncrasies were not tolerated; and thus discussion of profoundly personal questions — e.g., religion or sexuality — was taboo. Politics had the sole function of preserving order and the status quo, so that business could be conducted as usual. The burghers were thus the staunchest supporters of the nationalist idea, to which the aristocracy was soon to be won over as well once particularism ceased to be profitable. The new bourgeoisie contributed a strong belief in science and progress as the new faith, and in social Darwinism as the new ethic. Accordingly, only scientific knowledge — demonstrable concretely and logically — was considered valid and worth discussing. Human progress was felt to be clearly manifested in technological and industrial advances. And the justification for imperialism, power politics and for the insistence on self-reliance — rather than on social benefits — found its apology in Darwin's theory (translated into social terms) of the survival of the fittest. The teaching of all these values was carefully provided for: the traditional family structure, the state-controlled schools, and the military (1-3 years compulsory active duty for all males) were responsible for inculcating and reinforcing them in the youth of the nation.

Thus, all seemed neatly organized and provided for in this society. And yet, it was exactly these values which contributed significantly to the very mood of crisis that threatened them, for they helped to aggravate the polarization of German society into inimical groups: the privileged and the deprived, the contents and the malcontents. The poles varied in nature. There were those who could not meet the severe prerequisites for participation: the suicide rate among *Gymnasium* pupils rose alarmingly in the period.[15] Others fought them. Women, for example, began demanding more rights. The outcasts (the prostitutes, the mentally disturbed, the poor, the deviants, the political extremists, the rebellious artists) were becoming too numerous to be comfortably ignored.

CHAPTER 4

Poetry and Life in Expressionism

THE few months on the eve of the First World War were intensely productive ones for two young Expressionist artists living together in Dresden. The painter-poet Ludwig Meidner (1884-1966) and his close friend, the poet and occasional sketcher Ernst Wilhelm Lotz (1890-1914), had left the "turbulent and thousand-voiced" Berlin in search of quieter surroundings in which to work and investigate the world within themselves. They came to Dresden in the late spring of 1914, took a small apartment in the Bautzner Strasse, and set about their task. They worked side by side, Meidner at his easel and Lotz over his sketchbook or at his desk, taking turns firing up each other's imagination and encouraging each other's artistic daring. "We were of the same mind in everything," Meidner recalled in a report which was written shortly afterwards.[1] Their creative mood was almost frenzied: "We battled our way frantically through each day." And Meidner adds: "Lotz wrote his best poems now, and I sank down into the eccentricities of a godless, funereal world." The busy streets of Dresden outside their window, with their manifold sights and sounds, formed the backdrop to their work. They rushed into them when their creative excitement could no longer be contained: "We flared up together like a giant fire and ran speechless from the house." In the Dresden streets and one of its cafés they also renewed their "creative strength" and gathered up new inspiration for their canvasses and poems. Thus, as Meidner suggests, "fragments of the city, street-lamps and people" found their way into his work of this period, as they did also into the verses of Lotz, "winged singer of the sea of cities" as his friend called him.

Meidner's report on his sojourn with Lotz in Dresden was published in June, 1918, while the Expressionist movement was still very much alive; it is thus much more manifesto than memoir. But the work of both artists done around this time corroborates the report's historical verity concretely. Their experience, along with the work that came of it — especially the poetry Lotz completed around this time — provides some profound insights into the nature of Expressionism as a literary movement.

The poetry in question is contained in a collection Lotz prepared for publication during the summer of 1914. But Lotz was not allowed to see it into print himself; he fell in battle on Germany's western front in the first weeks of the war. The collection finally appeared two years later (fall, 1916) in a major Expressionist series under the title *Wolkenüberflaggt (Our Banner the Clouds).*[2] The poet's widow, Henny Lotz, reported in an afterword to the volume that the poems in it were "largely" written in her husband's last year of life.[3] Although most of them are typical of Expressionism in their exuberance and revolutionary zeal, it is the four poems in the cycle comprising the last section, "Jugend" ("Youth"), that are of particular interest for our purposes. In a highly original poetic language, and in a conceptual manner typical for the Expressionists, they set forth the development of revolutionary youth through four stages; in the process, they foreshadow a stage of the movement which Lotz was not allowed to know or share in himself because of his premature death.

The first poem, "Hart stossen sich die Wände in den Strassen..." ("The Walls are Jammed Together in the Streets..."), represents the stage of adolescence and emotional awakening. It opens by reestablishing for this cycle the modern urban setting that dominates the whole of *Wolkenüberflaggt:*

> Hart stossen sich die Wände in den Strassen,
> Vom Licht gezerrt, das auf das Pflaster keucht,
> Und Kaffeehäuser schweben im Geleucht
> Der Scheiben, hoch gefüllt mit wiehernden Grimassen.

> The walls are jammed together in the streets,
> Pulled by the light that strains to reach the pavement.
> And coffeehouses hover in the glimmer
> Of window panes, filled high with neighing grimaces.

There follows an expression of all the vague and ineffable yearnings of the flesh that always beset youth at this age:

Wir sind nach Frauen krank, nach Fleisch und Poren,
Es müssten Pantherinnen sein, gefährlich zart,
In einem wild gekochten Fieberland geboren.
Wir sind versehnt nach Reizen unbekannter Art.

Wir sind nach Dingen krank, die wir nicht kennen.
Wir sind sehr jung. Und fiebern noch nach Welt.
Wir leuchten leise. — Doch wir können brennen.
Wir suchen immer Wind, der uns zu Flammen schwellt.

We are sick for women, for flesh and pores;
We must have pantheresses, menacing and tender,
Born in a wild hot land of fever.
We are mad with longing for unknown temptations.

We are sick for things we do not know.
We're very young. And still have a feverish yearning
    for the world.
Our light glows softly. — Yet we could flare up.
We're always searching for the wind that fans us
    into flames.

The second poem in the cycle, "Wir wachen schon ein wenig heller auf..." ("We See More Clearly Now When We Awaken..."), already begins to establish the uniqueness and special isolation of these youths in their particular contemporary environment. As they now awaken intellectually as well as emotionally, they develop an awareness not only of their own potentials but also of the painful truths of the world about them:

Wir wachen schon ein wenig heller auf,
Wenn uns der Mittag um die Stirnen lodert,
Wir sind schon etwas kühner und heisser gespannt.
    . . .
Elektrisch fühlen wir: Wir sind da!
Wir können schon sehen.
Wir können verstehen.
Wir können schon zeichnen
In unsern Augen,
Hart und zum Schreien wahr.

We see more clearly now when we awaken
The heat of midday blazing round our brow;
We're more charged with heat and courage now.
. . .
Electrically we feel: we are alive!
We can see now.
We can comprehend.
We can sketch now
With our eyes,
Sharply and with painful truth.

They fuse their discernment of life's pain with its inherent joys
("our yes") in a determination, a "will" to fulfill themselves; and
their determination is fostered by fellowship with like-minded in-
dividuals ("our brothers"):

Und unterscheidend, entscheiden wir uns:
Wir haben uns unsre Verachtung gemerkt schneidend,
Und unser Ja.
Nachts,
Heimlich,
Kommen wir mit unsern Brüdern zusammen.
Wir haben den Wein aus dem Kreise verbannt:
Rausch ist unsre Gemeinsamkeit, unser Wunsch und das
    Schweben der Tat,
Beide umflackerten unsre Heimlichkeit.
Ein Wille schiesst aus uns. —Erblasst vom Warten:
Wir wissen schon den Tag. Wir fiebern schwer.
. . .

And discerning, we decide:
We will not forget the sting of our scorn,
And our yes.
At night,
In secret,
We assemble with our brothers.
We have banned wine from our circle:
Our intoxicant is our fellowship, our desire and our
    poised deed;
Both flickered round our secrecy like flames.
One will shoots forth from us. —Pale from waiting:
We know our day already. We are heavy with fever.

. . .

In "Die Nächte explodieren in den Städten..." ("The Nights Explode in the Cities..") they have become satiated with all that life (such as it is in their time) can offer them. The cities have bombarded them — like igniting explosives — with experiences and impressions:

> Die Nächte explodieren in den Städten,
> Wir sind zerfetzt vom wilden, heissen Licht,
> Und unsre Nerven flattern, irre Fäden,
> Im Pflasterwind, der aus den Rädern bricht.

> The nights explode in the cities;
> We are rent by the wild, hot light,
> And our nerves flutter, deranged strands,
> In the asphalt wind that whips out of the wheels.

These youths have known the intensity of revolutionary ideas:

> In Kaffeehäusern brannten jähe Stimmen
> Auf unsre Stirn und heizten jung das Blut,
> Wir flammten schon. Und suchen leise zu verglimmen,
> Weil wir noch furchtsam sind vor eigner Glut.

> In coffeehouses impetuous voices branded
> Our foreheads and fired up our young blood;
> We were aflame. And seek to die out softly,
> Because we are still fearful of our own fire.

They have experienced the kind of unfulfilling love that their materialistic world forces on them:

> Wir schweben müssig durch die Tageszeiten,
> An hellen Ecken sprechen wir die Mädchen an.
> Wir fühlen noch zu viel die greisen Köstlichkeiten
> Der Liebe, die man leicht bezahlen kann.

> We glide idly through the seasons of the day;
> At luminous corners we accost the girls.
> We still sense too much the hoary delights
> Of love which one can pay for easily.

Because they lack a sense of fulfillment and have not yet developed the courage to realize either themselves or the implicit goal of their revolutionary ideas, they drift "idly" through life, only consoled by the faith that they will some day attain the ideal:

> Wir haben uns dem Tage übergeben
> Und treiben arglos spielend vor dem Wind,
> Wir sind sehr sicher, dorthin zu entschweben,
> Wo man uns braucht, wenn wir geworden sind.

> We have surrendered to the day
> And drift guilelessly and playfully with the wind;
> We are quite certain that we will be
> Where we are needed when we have matured.

The final poem of the cycle, "Aufbruch der Jugend" ("Revolt of Youth"), is one of the most famous in all Expressionism. Having finally attained full maturity both intellectually and emotionally, and having cast off the lethargy of the past ("The lassitude which came over us in desolate nights...faded away..."), the young revolutionaries now rise up in organized insurrection:

> Also zu neuen Tagen erstarkt wir spannen die Arme,
> Unbegreiflichen Lachens erschüttert, wie Kraft, die
>   sich staut,
> Wie Truppenkolonnen, unruhig nach Ruf der Alarme,
> Wenn hoch und erwartet der Tag überm Osten blaut.
> Grell wehen die Fahnen, wir haben uns heftig entschlossen,
> Ein Stoss ging durch uns, Not schrie, wir rollen geschwellt,
> Wie Sturmflut haben wir uns in die Strassen der
>   Städte ergossen
> Und spülen vorüber die Trümmer zerborstener Welt.

> We flex our arms, full of strength for new days,
> Shaken by incomprehensible laughter, like strength
>   which is blocked,
> Like columns of troops, restless after the call to alarm,
> When the day long-awaited rises high across the East.

> Brightly waft our flags; our decision is fierce;
> A shock went through us; distress cried out; we charge
>   forth strong,
> Pouring like flood waters into the streets of the cities,
> Washing aside the ruins of a broken world.

They depose the tyrants of outmoded authority and free the oppressed and enslaved:

> Wir fegen die Macht und stürzen die Throne der Alten,
> Vermoderte Kronen bieten wir lachend zu Kauf,
> Wir haben die Türen zu wimmernden Kasematten zerspalten
> Und stossen die Tore verruchter Gefängnisse auf.

> We sweep aside authority and topple the thrones of
>   the elders;
> With laughter we offer up mouldering crowns for sale;
> We have broken down the doors to casemates resounding
>   with moans,
> And thrust open the gates of infamous prisons.

They envision themselves as the new Messiahs, "luminaries" who bring to mankind the salvation offered by the vision of a new and glorious world of fulfillment:

> Beglänzt von Morgen, wir sind die verheissnen Erhellten,
> Von jungen Messiaskronen das Haupthaar umzackt,
> Aus unsern Stirnen springen leuchtende, neue Welten,
> Erfüllung und Künftiges, Tage, Sturmüberflaggt!

> Illumed by the morning, we are the promised luminaries,
> Our youthful heads adorned with crowns of the Messiah;
> Bright, new worlds sprout forth from our minds,
> Fulfillment and future days; our banner a storm!

Thus, Lotz's "Jugend" seems like a poetic manifestation of his experience in Dresden as recorded more directly by Meidner. Even that last, strictly prophetic poem in the cycle probably found the concrete inspiration for its march of the revolutionaries through the city streets in Lotz's and Meidner's excited treks across Dresden. But we need not prove that these poems were indeed a record of this sort; there is so much of the general spirit of Expressionism in both Lotz's cycle and Meidner's reminiscence that the two documents were bound to agree with one another. Thanks to the typically Expressionist attitude that informs them, they also serve as an introduction to the movement.

I   *The Asphalt Streets*

First of all, there is in both documents the very strong urban background that either directly or indirectly informs all of Expressionism. Expressionist literature — like the other forms of artistic

expression represented in the movement — was profoundly a litera-
ture of the modern metropolis. Most Expressionists came from
such cities; the rest either moved to them or eventually spent most
of their time in them. The main centers of the movement were lo-
cated in the larger German cities: Berlin, Munich, Leipzig, Dres-
den. The foreign outposts of the Expressionists were similarly lo-
cated in other major European cities: Paris, Prague, Vienna,
Zurich. Here were based the large and influential circles of artists
and writers which functioned as the framework for attracting and
inspiring followers of the movement, as the organizers of its liter-
ary and extra-literary activities and as the sponsors of its many lit-
erary forums (journals, series publications, literary cabarets, pub-
lishing houses).

The city intruded into Expressionist literature as the basic
thematic underpinning. It put the Expressionists in direct touch
with modern life, its major concerns and questions. It thrust them
into the turbulent center of the great cultural upheaval outlined in
the previous chapter. In the cities they experienced firsthand the
great crises of life and thought of their time that sent them in search
of alternatives. As the compiler of a recently published anthology
of German poetry of the large cities has stated, "at no other time
have lyric poets devoted such intellectual intensity and personal
commitment to trying to grasp the nature of the large city and to
giving expression to it in poetic language."[4] Even quantitatively,
Expressionism is unique in this respect: no other body of literature
before or since has produced so many poems whose very theme is
the city. It appears again and again, even in the titles of poems:
"Die tote Stadt" ("The Dead City"), "Stadt, du steinernes
Ackerland" ("City, You Stone Field"), "Die Stadt der Qual"
("The City of Agony"), "Immanuel leidet in der grossen Stadt"
("Emmanuel Suffers in the Big City"), "Flucht aus der Stadt"
("Flight from the City"). Whole volumes of poetry were devoted
to this theme as well: Armin T. Wegner's *Das Antlitz der Städte
(The Face of the Cities,* 1917), Max Herrmann-Neisse's *Sie und die
Stadt (She and the City,* 1914), Sylvia von Harden's *Verworrene
Städte (Confused Cities,* 1919). Not surprisingly, the number of
poems written about Berlin in this period was legion: it was the
great, decisive experience for most Expressionists.[5]

Thus, it is clear that for the Expressionists the city was their true
milieu. As one of them so aptly put it, the city was the "asphalt
foundation" of their literature.[6] This was conspicuously the case

with their poetry. In the early stages of the movement, several of its spokesmen specifically called for a poetry with a clear urban base. In the context of such a declaration, published in early 1911 in *Der Sturm,* the influential theoretician and critic Kurt Hiller even argued against calling the new poetry by the traditional name of "Lyrik" ("lyric").[7] "Lyrik," he maintained, generally calls to mind a remoteness or snobbish aloofness from the real world; it thus best subsumes highly refined (Impressionist) poetry written by the likes of Stefan George or Rainer Maria Rilke. The new poets are quite different; they are "the poeticizers of our beloved and hated cities." They have a radically different mission from that of poets of the past, which Hiller defined this way:

I posit as the goal of the writing of a poem: the affective expression of that which the most cultivated type of man encounters daily. Thus: an honest poetic record of the thousands of small and great delights and sorrows in the life of the intellectual man of the cities.[8]

For Hiller, one of the masters of the urban-based poem was his friend, the Berlin poet Ernst Blass. Hiller wrote a very enthusiastic review (something he rarely did) of a volume of Blass's verse, *Die Strassen komme ich entlang geweht (I Come Drifting Down the Streets),* shortly after its appearance in the fall of 1912.[9] One poem in the collection had already been selected by Hiller for publication in an anthology he brought out in May of the same year.[10] This poem probably epitomized in Hiller's mind the kind of poetry he was advocating. It describes the emotional and intellectual sufferings of a dweller in the modern metropolis, driven to despair and fear by his loneliness:

Der Nervenschwache

Mit einer Stirn, die Traum und Angst zerfrassen,
Mit einem Körper, der verzweifelt hängt
An einem Seile, das ein Teufel schwenkt,
— So läuft er durch die langen Grossstadtstrassen.

Verschweinte Kerle, die die Strasse kehren,
Verkohlen ihn; schon gröhlt er arienhaft:
 Ja, ja — ja, ja! Die Leute haben Kraft!
Mir wird ja nie, ja nie ein Weib gebären

Mir je ein Kind!'' Der Mond liegt wie ein Schleim
Auf ungeheuer nachtendem Velours.
Die Sterne zucken zart wie Embryos
An einer unsichtbaren Nabelschnur.

Die Dirnen züngeln im geschlossnen Munde,
Die Dirnen, die ihn welkend weich umwerben.
Ihn ängsten Darmverschlingung, Schmerzen, Sterben,
Zuhältermesser und die grossen Hunde.[11]

The Neurasthenic

His forehead gnawed by dreams and fears,
His body hanging in despair
From a rope pulled by the devil
— Thus he runs through the long big-city streets.

The bastards who clean the streets
Mock him — and he shouts back his song:
''Yes, yes — yes, yes! The people are strong!
A woman will never, never bear

Me a child!'' The moon lies like slime
On a huge nocturnal velvet rug.
The stars twitch tenderly like embryos
On an invisible umbilical cord.

The strumpets' tongues entice us in closed mouths.
The strumpets who woo him weak and wiltingly.
He's tormented by twisting bowels, pains, dying,
The knives of pimps and the big dogs.

The poet Arthur Silbergleit seemed to be calling for a much more direct and detailed artistic record of the city in a manifesto entitled ''Die Stimme der Stadt'' (''The Voice of the City''), which was published just a few months after Hiller's in *Die Aktion*. Silbergleit characterizes the city as ''the harsh governess'' of his generation, into whose hands their mothers placed them because their mothers scarcely had the time to guide them in their first steps. And he expresses his desire to find an instrument capable of reproducing its myriad wild and turbulent sounds:

One would like to put the heart of the city up to one's ear like a sea shell, in order to listen to the hollow roar of the fables of life and the singing abysses of its seas. One would like to find a harp possessed of the most singular tones and capable of reproducing in sounds that wild vortex which enchants, amazes, stuns and overwhelms us: the thundering hymns of the thousands of electrical streetcars, the tight-rope tricks of the telpher-ways, the old idyl of the stage coach retold in the omnibusses, the green- and red-eyed frenzy of motorized vehicles racing along at apocalyptic speed, the rumbling cataracts of the taxicabs which are halted — miraculously — by the beckoning of a single human hand, the ardent dashing of commuter trains beneath bold arches that are bolder than the arches of vaulted cathedrals — one would like to capture the sounds of all things that attend our lives and fill our dreams.[12]

Silbergleit makes clear enough why the Expressionists were so preoccupied with the big city. In the large cities they were reminded daily of what made life in their century so different from the recent past. They were in the home of the modern world dominated by imposing man-made structures and machines. And Silbergleit reveals more clearly than Hiller that there were two sides to the city for the Expressionists. While they always found this new world impressive, they only rarely found it sanctionable. The ecstatic tribute to it in Ludwig Meidner's 1914 manifesto "Anleitung zum Malen von Grossstadtbildern" ("Guide to the Painting of Big-City Pictures") is exceptional:

We must begin at last to paint our homeland, the big city, which we love immensely. Our feverish hands should boldly sketch all the splendid and unusual, gigantic and dramatic features of the avenues, train stations, factories and towers on countless canvases, as large as frescoes.[13]

Most Expressionists primarily associated the city with the evils of modern life: coldness and insensibility, spiritual barreness, hardship and drudgery, corruption, the apparent venality of all things. Oskar Kanehl saw it as a place where "souls die and the brain celebrates grandiose victories." A visit to a large city (probably Berlin) in 1913, which Kanehl recorded that year in both an essay and a poem, very soon awakened in him a longing to return to the "unsullied sun" of his small hometown.[14] Berthold Viertel addressed the city with similar sentiments in a poem also published in 1913:

> . . .
> Ich nenne dich die Hölle der Verseuchten,
> Stadt ohne Seele aufgebaut.

Könnt ich entlaufen! Einen Acker haben,
Den nichts als Himmel überhängt.
Und dort nach meinem Herzen graben,
Das sich so tief hinabgesenkt.[15]

. . .

I call you the hell of the contaminated—
City constructed without soul.

If only I could escape. Have a field,
Covered only by the sky.
And there dig for my heart
That has sunken down so deep.

Johannes R. Becher and Martin Gumpert stressed the "misery"
that characterized life for them in the city, whereas poets like Blass
and Walter Rheiner stressed its loneliness.[16] Georg Heym, who
grew up in Berlin, wrote a number of poems about the city, in-
cluding three of the most famous poems of the period: "Die
Dämonen der Städte" ("The Demons of the Cities"), "Der Gott
der Stadt" ("The God of the City") and "Verfluchung der Städte"
("Execration of the Cities").[17] In often hallucinatory visions of an
ominous and doomed world, Heym personifies the city as an
autonomous, uncontrollable, demonlike force which visits death
and pestilence on its inhabitants. But probably the most desperate
and damning statements on the city in the period are those written
by Albert Ehrenstein in a poem about the city of his birth. He
writes of the degradation, the grief, and the selfishness of life in
Vienna, and closes with the angry petition to his readers to destroy
all the cities:

Ich bitte euch, zerstöret die Stadt,
Ich bitte euch, zerstöret die Städte:
Ich bitte euch, zerstört die Maschinen.
Aufreisset alle Wahnschienen!
Entheiligt ist euer Ort.
Euer Wissen ist nördliche Wüste,
Darin die Sonne verdorrt.

Ich beschwör euch, zerstampft die Stadt,
Zertrümmert die Städte,
Ich beschwör euch, zerstört die Maschine:
Ich beschwör euch, zerstöret den Staat![18]

> I beg you, destroy the city.
> I beg you, destroy the cities:
> I beg you, destroy the machines.
> Rip up all the rails of madness!
> This place is desecrated;
> Your knowledge is the desert of the north
> In which the sun is drying up.
>
> I implore you, trample this city under foot.
> Wreck the cities.
> I implore you, destroy the machine:
> I implore you, destroy the state!

The equation of the city with the modern world, so typical of Expressionism, seems to have become an especially conscious ingredient in Ehrenstein's poem. Yet, in spite of the Expressionists' frequent and sometimes unreserved condemnation of this new environment, they would have agreed with their contemporary, the painter August Macke, who claimed they had to incorporate its salient elements in their art if it was to become vital and new:

The new elements — automobile, commuter train, airplane, motion picture and machines — must produce a new artist, providing him with impressions which our Böcklins and Lenbachs did not have. The machine is conquering man. The artist must subordinate himself to this encroachment without sacrificing the Rhine, Mary in the Capitol, the Madonna with Vetch Blossom. This synthesis shall be our goal.[19]

II   *The Undaunted Generation*

Macke's strong sense of mission in that statement helps to explain the high pitch of excitement and enthusiasm in Lotz's "Jugend" and Meidner's "Erinnerung an Dresden." It is a mood that runs through most of the literature of the movement. It stems from the Expressionists' intense dedication to their work because they felt it had a purpose whose importance far transcended art itself. Unlike previous generations of painters and poets, they were not satisfied with just creating works of art; they required that these works also serve a higher function. In an age that was beginning to lose faith in most of its avowed values, the Expressionists stood for a rebirth of a profoundly idealistic faith in human potential and human endeavor. Their art manifests this faith patently, and generally also very programmatically ("littérature engagée"). For this reason

Max Brod has called them the "undaunted generation."[20]

The Expressionists saw the world from two perspectives. First of all, they sensed that all around them the old order was crumbling. Early Expressionist art and literature is filled with nightmarish, apocalyptic visions of some kind of impending catastrophe. In 1912 and 1913 Ludwig Meidner executed a series of canvases — some of them captioned "Apokalyptische Landschaft" (Apocalyptic Landscape") — which depict cities burning and crumbling under the impact of some undefined violence. Similar images abound in early Expressionist poetry. Erwin Loewenson, a spokesman of a circle of poets that called themselves "Der Neue Club" ("The New Club"), wrote in recalling the interests and activities of his group: "Our basic theme was the coming apocalypse which we already felt in our bones."[21] Autobiographical reports by members of Loewenson's circle and by numerous other Expressionists prove that this preoccupation was more than mere literary interest; it was based on a genuine fear or premonition. The finest poetic proof of Loewenson's claim is "Weltende" ("The World's End"), a poem composed probably about the middle of 1910 by a founding member of "Der Neue Club," Jakob van Hoddis. Besides being the most famous example of the apocalypse motif in Expressionism, it is also a poem which — in spite of its satirical overtones — had a powerful effect as prophecy and warning on its contemporary audience and fostered many imitations. It begins with a discomposing swipe at the narrow-mindedness ("pointed pate") of the Wilhelminian burgher, whose neatly organized world proceeds, in the alternatingly frightening (lines 2, 4, 5, 8) and droll (lines 3, 6, 7) images of the ensuing onslaughts, to come unstuck at its protective (roofs and dams) and supportive (bridges) joints. As typical in poems on this theme, the soruce of the disaster described is left mysteriously unidentified disposing the reader to conclude that it must be some immaterial force which is avenging itself for being neglected by a world obsessed with the material:

> Dem Bürger fliegt vom spitzen Kopf der Hut,
> In allen Lüften hallt es wie Geschrei.
> Dachdecker stürzen ab und gehn entzwei,
> Und an den Küsten — liest man — steigt die Flut.
>
> Der Sturm ist da, die wilden Meere hupfen
> An Land, um dicke Dämme zu zerdrücken.
> Die meisten Menschen haben einen Schnupfen.
> Die Eisenbahnen fallen von den Brücken.[22]

> A hat flies off a burgher's pointed pate;
> All winds are filled with screamlike sounds.
> Steeplejacks fall from roofs and break in two,
> And on the coasts — we read — flood waters rise.
>
> The storm has come; the seas run wild
> And hop on land, to squash fat dams.
> Most people have the sniffles.
> Railroad trains tumble from the bridges.

Some poets, like Hoddis and Heym, could do no more than shape such visions of impending doom. But most were like the Lotz of "Aufbruch der Jugend": they were also able to formulate an alternative order of their own making — whether meant for the world after the deluge or as a means of avoiding it. They blamed what many of them called the "spiritual lethargy" (or ethical indifference) of the ruling classes for the state of crisis their world was in, and were forced to assume, as they saw it, the full burden of responsibility for the future. A strong moral thrust, an emphasis on "ethics," is at the core of the whole movement and its literature. Responsibility, Carl Sternheim wrote in a manifesto for the new drama published on the eve of the war, stands above the poet's work as his guide in creation. Therefore, he continues, "the poet is the physician who attends to the ills of his times."[23] The aggressive or militant opposition of the movement to the ruling classes, the middle class in particular, is largely conditioned by this strong sense of responsibility. An unequivocal statement of this position was made at the very outset of the movement when Rudolf Kurtz formulated the program of *Der Sturm* in the opening pages of its premiere issue (March, 1910):

We do not want to entertain [our readers.] We want to cunningly demolish their slothful, gravely sublime world view. For we consider their gravity to be spiritual sloth, backwoods mustiness, whose psychology was defined long ago by Nietzsche.... The morality of brutal insensibility, which sees its lofty principles threatened by a slick paradox....

With the most provocative of gestures we shall ridicule any statements of this culture which aim at the retention of its conventions instead of the full appreciation of life.[24]

Significantly, the main bone which the Expressionists had to pick with the literature of the immediate past and with that of their opposing contemporaries (George, Hofmannsthal, Thomas Mann, Friedrich Lienhard, Gerhart Hauptmann, Paul Heyse, Paul Ernst, et al.) was not aesthetic; first and foremost, their criticism was levelled against its failure to take a direct and decisive stand on important moral issues of broader than purely literary implications.

I have already cited Hiller's and Pinthus's attacks on Impressionism. This stance was not restricted to the program of the movement; it also directly informed the poetry. Stadler's ''Form ist Wollust'' (''Form is Pleasure,'' 1914) can be interpreted as a poetic rendering of this critical position. The poem is part of a cycle, in which Stadler describes the poet's development out of the lethargy of aestheticism into the active commitment of the revolutionary. In ''Form ist Wollust'' he rejects the security and peace of a noncommittal life, which restricts expression, sensibilities, and experience (lines 3, 5, 7 below). He seeks instead a broader spectrum of experience (lines 1-2, 4, 6), which embraces all of mankind — even the outcast and destitute — and all of life:

> Form und Riegel mussten erst zerspringen,
> Welt durch aufgeschlossene Röhren dringen:
> Form ist Wollust, Friede, himmlisches Genügen,
> Doch mich reisst es, Ackerschollen umzupflügen.
> Form will mich verschnüren und verengen,
> Doch ich will mein Sein in alle Weiten drängen —
> Form ist klare Härte ohn' Erbarmen,
> Doch mich treibt es zu den Dumpfen, zu den Armen,
> Und in grenzenlosem Michverschenken
> Will mich Leben mit Erfüllung tränken.[25]

> Form and bolt had first to break,
> World to penetrate through opened channels:
> Form is pleasure, peace, heavenly sufficiency,
> But I am eager to plow up clods of earth.
> Form wants to bind and restrict me,
> But I want to force my being into all expanses —
> Form is clear hardness without pity,
> But I am driven to the gloomy, to the poor,
> And in boundless self-giving
> Life wants to still my thirst with fulfillment.

In the programmatic vocabulary of these artists, the ethical commitment that motivated their movement was expressed in a variety of concepts, each claiming to be a prime constituent of the Expressionist revolutionary personality: "Geist" ("spirit"), "Gesinnung" ("mental attitude"), "Gefühl" ("feeling"), "Intensität" ("intensity"), "Bewegung" ("action"), "Vision" ("vision"), and, in the latter stages of the movement, "Aktivismus" ("activism"). All of these concepts were used with strong moral overtones.

In one of the most influential manifestoes of the whole period, "Geist und Tat" ("Spirit and Action"), Heinrich Mann set forth the prerequisites for a long-awaited German revolution which was to free the Germans from the iron fist of absolute authority. The fusion of "spirit" and "action" in the potential leaders of the revolution was to result in the "ratio militans" of which all democratic movements are born.[26] Arthur Kronfeld, a poet and psychiatrist associated with Expressionists in Heidelberg and Berlin, identified manifesto published in early 1914 in the Heidelberg journal *Die Argonauten (The Argonauts):*

The primary quality of a revolution lies neither in a style nor a method; neither in a feeling nor a movement. . . . The mental attitude alone is what constitutes a revolution. . .the principle of all revolutions is the ethical attitude.[27]

For Kandinsky, a leading painter and theoretician of the "Blaue Reiter" ("Blue Rider") circle in Munich, the basic, artistic spirit of the middle class was "Ruhe" ("repose," "silence"). In Kandinsky's view this had moral implications: the burghers' spiritual inertia derived from their "self-satisfied, immovable, narrow" and uncreative world view. In *Concerning the Spiritual in Art* Kandinsky formulated an elaborate, opposing program which was to produce intensive "action" in art through certain color contrasts dictated by the artist's "innere Notwendigkeit" ("inner necessity").[28] Pinthus used "intensity" and "radicalism" in a 1919 statement to describe the spirit that drew Expressionists together and gave their ethically oriented revolution a common base:

This common factor is the intensity and radicalism of feeling, of mental attitude, of expression, of form; and this intensity, this radicalism forces poets in turn to oppose the race of men of the epoch now in decline and to prepare for and demand the new, better mankind they have long awaited.[29]

For Kasimir Edschmid, who wrote lengthy manifestoes which synthesized most previous pronouncements in the final years of Expressionism, the reliance upon "feeling" as the guiding principle produced a movement whose goal was to reshape the world as much as it was to revolutionize art.[30] Hiller defined political "activism," of which he was the foremost exponent after 1914, as the "morality of activity."[31] Finally, Ludwig Rubiner, another major voice in support of direct political action, drew together most of the positions just summarized in a widely read essay, published in 1917: "Der Mensch in der Mitte" ("Man in the Center"). "Intensity" of lifestyle, as Rubiner interpreted it here, is an ethical principle when governed by "spirit," because it alone can overcome the "lethargy" of the contemporary world and thereby realize a better society.[32]

III   Man in the Center

A key thesis in Rubiner's essay is alluded to in its title; it is one that provides us with as much critical insight into the unique nature of Expressionism as it must have provided his book with rhetorical impact. Rubiner's goal is a world in which the individual can realize more completely his own individuality. "Intensity" of lifestyle is, in this sense, already a starting point. In setting out to achieve this goal, individual man stands "in the center" in two respects: his needs are the center of interest, and his efforts are the center of activity in the revolution. As always in the Expressionist perspective, the individual is thrust into the center of the world, from which the dominant materialistic, scientific view of the period was trying to remove him. Expressionism is one of the first of the emphatically anthropocentric movements of our century. Man created by himself the technological world that surrounded and overwhelmed these young artists in the modern cities; and they profoundly believed that man could, if he wanted, create a far better world. This is why, as I shall discuss in more detail later, the Expressionist is always reminding us that he is the author of his work by placing the clear, self-conscious mark of his hand into the very substance of his canvases and literary texts, in the form of some significant deviation from established aesthetic norms (representational distortions, abstraction, unusual syntax, hyper-condensed language, incongruous imagery, etc.).

The orientation of the Expressionist world view around an optimistic dedication to individual potential and responsibility contributes to the strong rhetorical tone of the literature. In the poetry, this element explains the great predominance of highly tendentious verse. Its tendentious tone probably accounts for the failure of most Expressionist poetry to outlast its own age. This is very notably the case when its tone lapses conspicuously into sermonizing, as in Stadler's "Der Spruch" ("The Maxim," 1914), which closes with a phrase borrowed from the epigrams of the Baroque mystical poet and sometime priest Angelus Silesius (Johannes Scheffler). The poem also illustrates the Expressionist's central concern with man:

> In einem alten Buche stiess ich auf ein Wort,
> Das traf mich wie ein Schlag und brennt durch meine Tage fort:
> Und wenn ich mich an trübe Lust vergebe,
> Schein, Lug und Spiel zu mir anstatt des Wesens hebe,
> Wenn ich gefällig mich mit raschem Sinn belüge,
> Als wäre Dunkles klar, als wenn nicht Leben tausend wild
>   verschlossne Tore trüge,
> Und Worte wiederspreche, deren Weite nie ich ausgefühlt,
> Und Dinge fasse, deren Sein mich niemals aufgewühlt,
> Wenn mich willkommner Traum mit Sammethänden streicht,
> Und Tag und Wirklichkeit von mir entweicht,
> Der Welt entfremdet, fremd dem tiefsten Ich,
> Dann steht das Wort mir auf: Mensch, werde wesentlich![33]

> In an old book I came upon a phrase;
> It hit me like a blow and burns on through my days:
> And when I yield to dull delights,
> Prefer sham, deceit and show to essence,
> When I'm inclined to delude myself with hasty thoughts,
> As though obscurity were clear, as though life held not
>   a thousand wild barred gates in store,
> And repeated words, whose scope I've never sensed,
> When a welcome dream strokes me with velvet hands,
> And day and reality flee from me,
> Estranged from the world, alien to my deepest self,
> Then this phrase appears to me: Man, yield to your essence!

Like Lotz's "Aufbruch der Jugend," the bulk of Expressionist verse reads as though it was meant to be poetic manifesto. *Kameraden der Menschheit (Comrades of Mankind)* is an anthology of some of the most aggressively tendentious verse of the movement. The volume appeared in the spring of 1919, shortly after the

November Revolution.[34] Its editor, Rubiner, opened his afterword with a statement that can, to some degree, be applied to all Expressionist poetry:

Each poem in this book is a commitment by its author to the fight against an old world, to the march into the new human country of the social revolution. A commitment which was made at a time when it still endangered the personal security of its author. And therewith some poets of our time have finally done what was so remote from the literature of the previous generation: they have courageously accepted responsibility.[35]

So strongly did a sense of commitment inform Expressionist poetry that it gave rise to a virtually new subgenre: the utopian poem. The utopian poem had always been a rarity in literature, no doubt because of the basic unsuitability of a theme as broad as the vision of an ideal world for such a concise and opaque medium as the lyric. In Expressionism, however, it achieved a surprising level of popularity. The third section of Rubiner's anthology opens with the utopian poem "Vorbereitung" ("Preparation") by Johannes R. Becher, with whom this type of poem was a special favorite. "Vorbereitung" has been frequently reprinted, probably because it so directly expresses the ethical posture of Expressionism. It is the poet himself who is both the subject and the "I" of Becher's poem. Expressionism once more promoted the ancient conception of the poet as "poeta magus," "vates," or seer, last revived in Germany on such a broad scale by the Romantics in a similar age of crisis. For the Expressionists, the poet's special perceptiveness and sensibility make him once again the voice of truth and the prophet of the ideal. And so in "Vorbereitung" he is both the bearer of the vision of the "new world" and the leader of the revolution that is to pave the way for it:

Der Dichter meidet strahlende Akkorde.
Er stösst durch Tuben, peitscht die Trommel schrill.
Er reisst das Volk auf mit gehackten Sätzen.

Ich lerne. Ich bereite vor. Ich übe mich.
Wie arbeite ich — hah leidenschaftlichst! —
Gegen mein noch unplastisches Gesicht —:
Falten spanne ich.
Die Neue Welt
(— eine solche: die alte, die mystische, die Welt der
Qual austilgend —)

Zeichne ich, möglichst korrekt, darin ein.
Eine besonnte, eine aüsserst gegliederte, eine *geschliffene*
    Landschaft schwebt mir vor,
Eine Insel glückseliger Menschheit.
Dazu bedarf es viel. (Das weiss er auch längst sehr wohl.)

O Trinität des Werks: Erlebnis Formulierung Tat.[36]

The poet eschews resplendent chords.
He blasts on tubas and shrilly whips his drum.
He stirs the people up with rough-hewn lines.

I'm learning. I'm preparing. I'm practicing.
Oh how I work — yes, most passionately! —
On my still formless face:
I span folds.
The New World
(— one that obliterates the old, the mystical, the world
    of agony —)
I sketch upon it, as accurately as possible.
I envision a sunny, a carefully organized, a *sculptured*
    country,
An island of blissful mankind.
Much is required to achieve it. (For long he has known
    this very well.)

O trinity of creation: experience formulation deed.

The conciseness of Becher's language does not allow him to tell us what specifically must be done to attain utopia; we learn only that "much is required to achieve it" and that the general formula for action resembles Heinrich Mann's "ratio militans": "O trinity of creation: experience formulation deed." Nor does Becher state in detail how his "new, blessed state" will look in reality, only that it will be "sunny, a carefully organized, a perfectly developed country" and that a "blissful mankind" will reside in it. But the main purpose of the many Expressionist manifesto poems resembling this one is hardly to instruct in specifics. Rather, they all seek to inspire the reader to action, to participation. And so the conclusion of the utopian poem is most critical:

— Lasst uns die Schlagwetter-Atmosphäre verbreiten! —
Lernt! Vorbereitet! Übt euch!

— Let us spread an explosive atmosphere! —
Learn! Prepare! Practice!

IV   *The World as Vision*

We can see quite clearly in Becher's "Vorbereitung" ("I envision a sunny, a carefully organized, a perfectly developed country...."), as we saw earlier in Lotz's "Wir wachen schon ein wenig heller auf..." ("One will shoots forth from us.") that the inner world of the Expressionist is the source of his ideal conception of the outer world. Theodor Däubler, an Expressionist poet and champion of Expressionist painting, wrote in 1916: "Our age has a grand design: a new eruption of the soul. The self creates the world."[37] This is what the term "Expressionism" seeks to suggest. In contrast to the Impressionist, who allowed the basic content of his art to be dictated by external impressions, the Expressionist wants to project — to "express" — his internal vision into the external world, imposing on it the shape and substance of his self. Stadler's admonition "Man, yield to your essence!" in "Der Spruch" is informed by a related insistence on the primacy of the self over the deceptiveness and frivolousness of external reality.

The Expressionists reacted directly to their contemporary sociopolitical reality; but when they formed their opposing ideality, they based it on a mental conception rather than a visual perception. Edschmid defined this orientation in a famous manifesto, first delivered as a lecture in December, 1917 in Berlin:

Thus, the whole perceptual space of the Expressionist artist becomes vision. He does not see; he intuits. He does not describe; he shapes. He does not receive; he seeks. Now there is no longer a series of facts: factories, houses, sickness, whores, screaming and hunger. Now there is the vision of them.[38]

The Expressionists considered the contemporary "middle-class and capitalist" reality (as Edschmid called it) to be only the currently dominant reality. For them it was an "imaginary reality" — an artificial, arbitrary construct of man, a by-product of the new natural sciences and the "scientific method." The scientific approach to nature, based on the systematic, logical analysis of gathered data, had destroyed the spiritually oriented world of the Middle Ages, centered in God, and replaced it with a physically oriented world, centered in nature. Its physiognomy was strictly material, shaped by the technology which the new sciences had made possible. Its system of values was at the core material, based on the accumulation of wealth that the new sciences had accelerated. Materialism was the new world view; all verities were ultimately tangible.

The aim of this new world was ostensibly to make life more pleasurable. But as the Expressionists saw it, this aim was doomed to defeat from the start. It was based on a myopic, one-sided view of life which felt called upon to satisfy only the superficial (tangible) material needs of man and to activate only his logical thought apparatus. Moreover, they believed that the technology which this approach to the world had fostered had become autonomous, dominating rather than palliating the life of man, who had created it. The rights and needs of the individual had been neglected or suppressed, and, through the competitive atmosphere nurtured by this world view, men had been put at odds with one another. Pinthus described these developments in an essay we have cited before:

He [man] allows thought and action, government and family life to be controlled by this imaginary reality more harshly and humiliatingly than they ever were before by the most absolute monarchy or the most orthodox religion.[39]

Therefore, Pinthus goes on, Expressionism was a "spiritual fight against that imaginary reality." Most of his fellow theorists wrote in terms of a fight against a crass materialism that was stifling them. They wanted out of their society. René Schickele, the editor of *Die Weissen Blätter (The White Sheets),* wrote of the beginnings of the movement in 1920:

We were unhappy in the twilight of our era; we wanted out of a world that was making clever business deals with both heart and mind. We wanted to get away from military music and the homespun cultivation of feeling, whereby the beast in man is safely stored away. We were downtrodden, poor, ambitious, checkmated after only the third move, just as soon as we offered our ruling contemporaries the slightest challenge. We cried out.[40]

The narrow concerns of the materialistic world that Schickele describes divided existence and caused a "split in the personality" of man, as Gottfried Benn termed it.[41] Its emphasis on tangible life ignored all intangibles: man's deepest physical as well as his deepest spiritual longings. Both the erotic life and non-systematic thought were taboo.[42] Man, Benn declared in "Das moderne Ich" ("The Modern Self," 1920), was divided against himself and isolated in nature by a lopsided cerebralism, just as Narcissus had been by the light of self-awareness.[43]

The Expressionists rejected this "distorted image" of reality and set out in search of a more encompassing one. They pursued with a vengeance areas of thought and feeling skirted and shunned until their time: paradoxes, contradictions, incongruities, illogicality, insanity, distorted perspectives, brutal violence, eroticism, etc. By breaking through the façade of established reality (aesthetically, intellectually, socially), they sought to discover the other realities that lay beyond, to reveal the "heart," "essence," or "core" of all things beneath their conventional definitions. In this sense, Benn claimed Expressionism was a "demolition of reality...a ruthless penetration to the roots of things."[44] Pinthus wrote similarly: "The phenomena of reality are embraced, decomposed and recreated so as to grasp the essence, heart and nerves of things, so as to grasp simultaneously the core along with the outer shell...."[45] Encouraged, when not directly inspired or enlightened, by the writings of Nietzsche and Freud, they felt that this "core" or "essence" was to be found deep within man. The pursuit of the inner qualities therefore became the first concern of Expressionism.

Oskar Maria Graf wrote of the attitude of his circle of anarcho-Expressionist friends in Munich before the war:

The inner qualities of the self were the essential ones, and the task of the true anarchist was this: to develop his external life according to the law of the innermost urge — with the greatest of freedom, unrestricted, and as little affected, by "culture" as possible.[46]

Just as the Expressionists rejected hyper-rationalism because its excesses had corrupted and suppressed man's "inner qualities," so they also rejected standard psychology as "dilettantish" because they felt that it did not sufficiently respect those same qualities.[47] Psychology wanted only to classify and categorize man's inner workings and to force him into stereotypes of behavior. For this reason, Paul Kornfeld argued against the psychological ("naturalistic") style of acting in a 1918 manifesto for the Expressionist theater. He claimed that it reduced the actor and the character he was portraying to a "mechanism."[48] Edschmid maintained that the Expressionist rejects psychology because it does not represent a "direct experience" of life, only the "analysis" of it.[49]

Psychoanalysis, on the other hand, was embraced by the Expressionists without reservation. They believed, as Alfred Döblin put it in 1913, that psychoanalysis is "the only science which deals with the total psyche of man."[50] This new science seemed to them to delve much more deeply than psychology could into human character, and they felt that its aim was not to classify and then treat routinely, but to heal through simple understanding. Max Picard, writing for an Expressionist almanac published in 1919, seemed almost to want to reduce the difference between psychology and psychoanalysis to an opposition between deductive and inductive reasoning:

The Expressionist is therefore not psychological; he is psychoanalytical. This is not a contradiction. On the contrary: psychology proceeds from *one* thing to a thousand things; psychoanalysis proceeds from a thousand things to one. It sifts through a thousand disparate experiences until *one* tendency is found in them which can be traced to one *single* experience.[51]

Picard's real point, of course, is that the final aim of psychoanalysis and Expressionism is the same. The psychoanalyst tries to harmonize human personality by searching for the single, unifying experience; Expressionism strives to reunify existence by reintegrating the various forces in the human personality divided by the materialist world view. The Expressionists state this will to unity in a variety of ways, but the ultimate goal is always the same.

The conception of the new unity among the Expressionists was sometimes very general. Pinthus and Carl Einstein described it simply as the act of embracing the "totality of being."[52] Sternheim shared this view and detailed two requisite conditions to realizing the sense of totality which owe a conspicuous debt to Nietzsche: man must adopt an attitude of complete "objectivity" toward the multiplicity of things in life, refusing to weigh them against traditional notions of "good" or "evil", and he must cultivate his own individuality without restriction (an act Sternheim called "Privatcourage," the courage to assert oneself aggressively).[53] In a similar vein, Edschmid maintained that the expressionist could heal the "rent state" of contemporary existence by combining an intense expression of his innermost feelings with "a great, all-encompassing compassion for the world."[54] Members of the *Sturm* circle (Herwarth Walden, Lothar Schreyer, Otto Nebel) frequently theorized about a "unity of being" that could be achieved by eliminating the dominance of the logical faculty in man as established by the Enlightenment. Man would thereby be reintegrated into the cosmos.[55] Heinrich Vogeler was one of many Expressionists who saw the solution to the tragic divisions in the world and man to lie in a quite traditional means, which he called "active love," the practicing of a deep concern for the well-being of one's fellow man through concerted action.[56]

Very often adherents of the movement stated this ultimate goal in specifically psychoanalytical terms. The most outspoken and influential of these was the highly volatile revolutionary Otto Gross, a promising student of Freud in Vienna before he joined the Expressionist camp in Munich and Berlin prior to the war. Gross boldly fused two major breakthroughs in man's development: what he called "the unparalleled transvaluation of all values" that was initiated by Nietzsche and Freud's continuation of it in his discoveries of the deep recesses of the human psyche. He then attempted to place this radical synthesis in the service of the cultural revolution launched by the Expressionists. In a key statement in 1913, entitled "Zur Überwindung der kulturellen Krise" ("Towards the Overcoming of the Cultural Crisis"), he declared:

The psychology of the unconscious is the philosophy of the revolution, i.e., it is destined to be that, because it is the ferment of revolt within the psyche, the liberation of the individual from the bonds of his own unconscious. It is destined to make us capable of being free inwardly, destined to be the preliminary stage of the revolution.[57]

As Gross interpreted it, psychoanalysis is a practical, empirical method for gaining profound self-knowledge. This self-knowledge will heal the divisive conflict between the unconscious and the conscious precipitated by the harsh demands of the external world in early childhood. The result will be a "new ethics," which will free the individual from the repression of higher authority (most tangibly represented by patriarchal privilege), provide for a freer and happier relationship between the sexes and will allow for "the full harmonious development of the highest innate potentials of each individual."

Most often the Expressionist's striving for unity in an age of great divisions is expressed within the conceptual framework of Nietzsche's dialectical monism.[58] As Benn once suggested in the most glowing of the many Expressionist tributes to this philosopher, Nietzsche was the one great mentor of the movement, the source for all that Benn's generation "discussed...thought through...suffered through; one could also say expatiated upon."[59] Nietzsche, Benn summarized, "had given the definitive formulations; all the rest was exegesis."

Nietzsche's monistic ideal of unity centers on a synthesis of the Apollonian and Dionysian principles. He first expounded these two principles in *The Birth of Tragedy,* and although his interpretation of the Dionysian later changed, the nature of the synthesis remained the same to the end. In *The Birth of Tragedy,* the Apollonian embodies the form-giving, structuring, organizing, or restraining force in man. It is broadly identifiable with conscious thought, or even, in the extreme, with reason. Its polar principle is the Dionysian, which embodies the force of destructiveness, dissolution, formlessness, ceaseless desiring, abandonment. It encompasses the area of the human psyche associated with the unconscious and passion. In Nietzsche's mind, the dominance of either principle is uncreative and unfulfilling; only the synthesis or balance of the two — which he was eventually to label the "will to power" — can provide man with a truly satisfying existence.[60]

The role of Nietzsche as a leading prophet and mentor of the movement was nowhere as prominently enforced and advertised as in "Der Neue Club," the first Expressionist circle of poets to develop a distinct identity. Hiller, Loewenson, Blass, and Erich Unger were formulators of its program. Nietzsche was clearly their ideological source. He came willy-nilly to the club's defense whenever it needed convincing support. His works were avidly read and discussed by the club's members, recited at their formal literary evenings, and widely quoted in their own writings. The club's central concept of "new pathos" is hardly imaginable without the impetus of Nietzsche's synthetic will to power.

The phrase "new pathos" was borrowed from the title of an important manifesto by Stefan Zweig, first published.in 1909, the same year in which "Der Neue Club" was founded. It was snatched up by the club's members and used as the label for a philosophy aimed at a "regeneration" of contemporary society. They believed that society was heading for some kind of catastrophe because it lacked cultural vitality: it was oppressed from within by spiritual lethargy and rent apart intellectually from without by a civilization that had grown at too fast a pace for man to be able to assimilate it properly. Man had been robbed of the "centrality" of character he had enjoyed in an earlier age. The "new pathos" would stimulate a revitalization of modern society through restoration of a "perspective of totality" and a "total synthesis" of human character. The club's pathos was called "new" because it was not just an arousal of feeling but also a stirring up of the mind. Loewenson wrote:

Our "new pathos" was, first of all, like any pathos a stirring up — but not only of feeling, as with the old, intellectually dependent and therefore all the more empty sounding "pathetics".... It was also a new kind of pathos which did not exclude the intellect....[61]

The "new pathos" is thus equivalent to an overt expression of Nietzsche's "will to power," a synthesis of mind and body, of feeling and thought. Hiller called it the "Hellenic ideal of harmony." He saw the source of the division in contemporary man's character in the attempt to absorb an overly refined culture "quantitatively" through logical analysis and categorization (i.e., through the natural-scientific method). However, Hiller maintained, such a culture could only be grasped instinctively; and to do this, man must bring both sides of his basic nature, his rational and nonrational faculties, into equilibrium. The result would then be the "synthetic refinement of the totality of a psychical being":

If the idea of the "cultured" individual is fulfilled in this way, with the simple ethos of refinement accompanied by the demand that this refinement become a basic property of all experience, of *all* activity, that it permeate one's character, that — instead of being limited to thought alone, or to feeling alone, or to sociological behavior alone, or to some other capability — it become *universal:* then the formula "culture" will be transformed into a term of the highest praise that we can pay an individual except for that for creative power.... Art, knowledge, experience and problem solving, feeling and thought embrace one another, mingle and blend with one another in such restless intensity, with such chemical force that the so-called "classicistic" requirement that the two functions be developed in strict separation, in peaceful co-ordination, without the one "intruding" into the territory of the other...seems like a constraint.[62]

Else Lasker-Schüler's masterful poem "Ein alter Tibetteppich" ("An Old Tibetan Carpet," 1910) illustrates in poetic terms how the Expressionist "decomposes" the fabric of conventional reality so as to be able to create in its place a higher, more unified cosmos. The poem was no doubt inspired by her relationship with Karl

Kraus, the editor of the Viennese journal *Die Fackel (The Torch),* whom she called in her poetic fantasy world "The Dalai Lama" (see the reference below to "sweet lama's son"):

> Deine Seele, die die meine liebet,
> Ist verwirkt mit ihr im Teppichtibet.
>
> Strahl in Strahl, verliebte Farben,
> Sterne, die sich himmellang umwarben.
>
> Unsere Füsse ruhen auf der Kostbarkeit,
> Maschentausendabertausendweit.
>
> Süsser Lamasohn auf Moschuspflanzenthron,
> Wie lange küsst dein Mund den meinen wohl
> Und Wang die Wange buntgeknüpfte Zeiten schon?[63]
>
> Your soul, which is in love with mine,
> Is intertwined with it in the Carpet of Tibet.
>
> Ray within ray, enamored of their colors,
> Stars, which wooed each other all heaven long.
>
> Our feet rest upon its preciousness,
> Thousands upon thousands of stitches wide.
>
> Sweet lama's son on musk plant throne,
> How long have your lips been kissing mine
> And cheek to cheek in the gaily colored fabric of the ages?

As is typical in Lasker-Schüler's poetic world, love in this poem is the medium through which both contemporary reality can be transcended (in Pinthus's phrasing: "decomposed") and the whole of existence harmonized. Love is clearly the link with the divine, with God (line 4). And it is the mainstay in an intimately integrated and fully homogeneous cosmos, symbolized by the radiant and parti-colored carpet in which the lovers are intertwined and from which they are inseparable (lines 1-3). Love is also the link to eternity's boundlessness, for absolute freedom is acquired through love. It is freedom from the limitations of space: the carpet on which the lovers stand and into which they are interwoven is endless, limitless, encompassing the total universe (lines 5-6). And it is freedom from the restrictions of time as well: this is suggested in the reference to "all heaven long" (line 4) and the "gaily colored fabric of the ages," which corresponds to the multi-colored carpet and the "colors" of the lovers (line 9). Finally, sensual love (lines 7-9) and spiritual love (line 4) are fused harmoniously. Thus, in Lasker-Schüler's vision there are no longer any divisions: neither between body (which is otherwise bound to space and time) and soul (which is always ethereal), nor between the inner and the outer world of man.

For Lasker-Schüler, the ancient, non-European cultures from Egypt to Tibet were the sources of the lost ideal of harmony. But when the Expressionists searched the past for models for the present, most cast a respectful glance back at Hellenic Greece, as Hiller did in the essay quoted earlier. Some forty years before them, Nietzsche's philological studies had led him to a discovery that the closest approach to his ideal had occurred in the character of the Hellenes. His view was echoed by many voices among his Expressionist followers. Anselm Ruest, a poet and essayist from the circle around Alfred Richard Meyer's publishing company in Berlin, outlined an aesthetic for Expressionist poetry in a dialogue in classical style, set in ancient Greece.[64] Apollodorus, Ruest's spokesman here, finds the exemplary foundation of the new poetry of contemporary Germany in the life and thought of Socrates, whose primary goal was the attainment of the "golden mean" — "the marriage of sensuality and cognition." Apollodorus says: [Socrates's] efforts were all, as I have often heard said of him, directed toward achieving the finest mixture, toward the mean, toward the mathematical marriage of sensuality and cognition."[65] By striving (unwittingly) to emulate the Greek philosopher, as Ruest's alter ego further suggests, the contemporary poets (Expressionists) are being freed inwardly from conventional notions of "good" and "evil" and therewith as well from the renunciation of the "flesh" in favor of an "incorporeal spirit." Outwardly, their Socratic efforts are manifested in a newly found ability to embrace openly all aspects of life and human experience, from the crassly physical to the sublimely spiritual. They are thereby able to overcome the "curse, which for thousands of years has made their bodies seem loathsome to them."[66]

For Benn, the flesh of man, not the chimeras of the mind, is in a related sense the unacknowledged core of existence. Benn found his great model for psychic unity in ancient Greece, too ("most luminous Greece" as he extolled it in "Das moderne Ich"). But he also found it in virtually all "Southern" (especially Mediterranean) civilizations. In these climes, he believed, man had not yet succumbed to the excesses of the intellect, the narcissistic cerebrations that had painfully isolated the man of the "North" from his natural origins. The way back to the Hellenic "joy" of harmonious being lay in an abandonment of the hyper-logical approach to reality fostered by the natural scientific mind. Man must revert atavistically to the perspective of "the primacy of the whole." He must learn to close his eyes and unconsciously "breathe in the fragrance of the warm forests," to scent the wind that comes from "deep within the deserts" of North Africa and "crosses the sea to the Levant." Man, Benn says, should "make love" rather than learn to collect specimens.[67] By embracing the whole of physical existence in such self-abandon, he will once more be harmoniously reintegrated into the totality of the cosmos.[68]

Whatever the terms used to state the ideal, one point the Expressionists all agreed upon was this: of the many forms of expression and endeavor at man's disposal, art could best manifest the vision of the ideal. So they put most of their energy into their artistic creations, convinced that they were thereby serving life best.

V *A Community of Artists*

Before concluding the present chapter and turning to an examination of the specific ways in which the Expressionists gave poetic expression to their vision of the ideal, I must return once more to Lotz's "Jugend" cycle and Meidner's "Erinnerung an Dresden." Meidner suggested in his reminiscence how productive a communal lifestyle could be for artists:

We were of the same mind in everything. We sparked each other's excitement constantly with our raptures — encouraged each other in all our daring exploits; and day after day we consented lightheartedly to each other's foolishness. — Poets and painters do not have to worry about working together. There is no enmity and jealousy. There is only luminous enrichment and life in spiritual profusion.[69]

Lotz made a similar "fellowship" of like-minded revolutionaries the very seedbed of the movement which he followed through to culmination in his cycle (see the poems "Hart stossen sich die Wände in den Strassen..." and "Wir wachen schon ein wenig heller auf..." cited above). Both of these testimonies indicate the overall importance of the sense and support of an artistic-ideological community in Expressionism. And they both document an important fact of the movement: there was no separation of art and life. Other revolutionary, avant-garde movements have known this phenomenon to a degree as well, of course: the Storm and Stress and Romanticism in Germany, Symbolism in France and England, the Beats in America. But probably at no other time have art and life been so intimately entangled as in German Expressionism. Not only were the lives of the Expressionists completely devoted to their art, their art was in equal measure suffused with the thought and content of their lives. To vary a statement by the distinguished American poet Wallace Stevens: literature was the better part of their lives and life the better part of their literature.[70]

In the poetry of Expressionism this phenomenon resulted in the development of what was to a significant extent a public poetry, i.e., a poetry written with a strong awareness of the audience and often intended to be read aloud. Zweig, who recorded this development at its very inception in the manifesto "Das neue Pathos," maintained that its most recent antecedent even predated recorded history.[71] Much as the American poet Kenneth Rexroth was to assess the similar public poetry of his fellow Beats many decades later, Zweig believed that the new poets of his time were beginning to establish once more the intimate, tribal relationship that had existed between poet and audience long ago.[72] Zweig found the origins of this development in the close proximity of large numbers of people in the new metropolises. As he quite correctly perceived, both the poet and his poetry had acquired a new character and function in this context. Like the public poets of past ages, the new poet was committed to a cause. His poetry was often read aloud before audiences in the literary cabarets that abounded in Expressionism. He stood now face to face with his audience. Since he would almost naturally want to move it directly, both he and his poem were more emotionally charged. But he would also want to convince; he therefore had to check and control his own emotions as well as those of his audience. He was thus both the "tamer and inciter of the audience's emotions." (Blass was similarly to claim, a few years later, that the new poet was a "thinker" as well as a "fighter": "This thinker will be very scrupulous and full of a sense of responsibility, yet fiery."[73]) The new poetry was thus very often a rhetorical poetry: it was inspired by a will to action and driven by a strong sense of moral responsibility. The poet was thus once again, Zweig believed, capable of becoming the "spiritual leader of his age."

Zweig was right. As the young Expressionists came of age, they began to feel alienated by their society. They were thrust together in the large cities and soon began to discover the fellowship of mind Lotz describes in his cycle, most often in the artist cafés of Germany's big cities. The cafés were the great meeting places of the Expressionists, who were drawn to them as to lone islands of dissent in an otherwise almost uniformly obedient society. Leonhard Frank summarized the importance of the artist café in the lives of the Expressionists in his autobiographical novel *Links, wo das Herz ist (On the Left, Where the Heart Is):*

In the two years since he had come to Munich he had learned a lot from Professor So-and-so at the art school and even more in the Café Stephanie through the daily — and most often night-long — discussions about God and the world and life. He had at first learned to follow in his mind what the others were discussing, and had experienced one day the sensation that he could think all alone at home on his own. Among other things, he had also learned in the bohemian café, where the conventional style of life was completely done away with, to see the things of life on their own terms and in a new way.[74]

The artist café was thus a place where these young poets and painters could act and talk as they wished without fear of censure. And it was also a place where they could work, sitting next to fellow Expressionists at their regular tables, inspiring each other, or sharing their efforts with their table companions and finding encouragement or advice. But they could not only enjoy a greater amount of freedom here than in most other places; as Frank suggests, they could even learn to think more independently than they could elsewhere. The café was both a place to meet supportive friends and a kind of ideological "exchange-office" (Max Krell), "a stock-exchange of ideas" (Lasker-Schüler), "a place of edification" (Hans Purrmann), and even a "school" where one could "learn to see, understand and think" (Wolfgang Goetz).[75] Leonhard Frank again makes a typical assessment when he refers to the artist café as his "university":

The Café Stephanie was his university where the results of contemplation were delivered up to him. And since fate had failed to provide him with the time and money for studying all the thousands of fat books, he had to work through all the preliminary stages of intellectual development on his own in order to acquire the final results. He had passed his exams at the university of the Café Stephanie and was now a professor with a teaching chair at the table near the stove.[76]

If the Expressionists were not always given as extensive an education in the café as Frank and others seem to have enjoyed, they were at least exposed here, in long, excited discussions with their acquaintances and friends, to the ideas and attitudes that gave substance and structure to their cultural revolution. Hiller lectured them here on the faults and failures of past literature; Walden instructed them in the aesthetics of the new painting; Salomo Friedländer expounded on Nietzsche; Gross taught them his original blend of revolutionary reform and Freudian theories on the human psyche; and in his angry diatribes, Pfemfert exposed the facts and fictions of Wilhelminian politics. These were all decisive lessons; they stuck in the students' minds, shaping both the style and the content of their work. As Richard Seewald recalls:

Whoever became a regular guest here had crossed the Rubicon of his life. Here he could either lay the foundation of his later fame or come to ruin. Here, in endless conversations that lasted for hours or all night, he could find or lose himself in the maze and confusion of the opinions and philosophies recited with religious fervor.[77]

Broadly considered, the café was the fertile soil in which both the ideological and the physical roots of Expressionism as a movement were put down. Here the Expressionists formed their circles, many of which had a formal, or at least a self-conscious, structure, such as Hiller's "Der Neue Club," Alfred R. Meyer's "Der schwarze Club" ("The Black Club"), the circle around the journal *Die Dichtung (Poetry)* and the Dadaist group active in Berlin at the close of the war.[78] The Expressionists founded and staged their literary recitals (cabarets) here: evenings sponsored, for example, by "Das neopathetische Cabaret" ("The Cabaret of the New Pathos"), "Das Cabaret Gnu" ("The Cabaret Gnu"), "Die feindlichen Brüder" ("The Inimical Brothers") and the journals *Die Aktion, Der Sturm, Neue Jugend (New Youth)* and *Die Neue Kunst (The New Art)*. The Expressionists met in the cafés with their publishers and planned or founded numerous publications (journals, series, almanacs, anthologies).

These publications were central to the life of Expressionist poetry, especially in the first two stages of the movement. First of all, such journals provided the new poets with almost the only public forum for their verse outside the cabarets where they recited it. Several gave special emphasis to the lyric by devoting whole issues to poetry, occasionally even to that of just one author. There were also several series publications that were established by Expressionist circles and that catered exclusively or primarily to the new poetry: e.g., Alfred R. Meyer's "Lyrische Flugblätter" ("Lyrical Broadsheets," 1907-23), "Der jüngste Tag" ("Judgment Day," 1913-22), "Lyrische Bibliothek" ("Lyrical Library," 1913-14), "Die Aktions-Lyrik" ("Action-Poetry," 1916-22), "Der rote Hahn" ("The Red Rooster," 1917-25) and "Das neueste Gedicht" ("The Newest Poem," 1918-20).[79] Finally, there were many anthologies of poetry generally sponsored by publishers from the Expressionist camp, which attracted much attention to the movement: e.g., *Der Kondor (The Condor,* 1912), edited by Hiller; *Neuer Leipziger Parnass (The New Parnassus of Leipzig,"* 1912), edited by Pinthus; *Kameraden der Menschheit (Comrades of Mankind,* 1919), edited by Rubiner; and the famous and frequently reprinted *Menschheitsdämmerung (Dawn of Mankind,* 1919-20), also edited by Pinthus.[80]

Just as these publications were all conceived of as alternatives to the established (conservative) literary tribunes that consistently rejected the Expressionists' work, so were the cafés alternatives to the conventional literary salons in which the Expressionists were similarly not welcome. More than any other institution in the period, the cafés were therefore both the training ground and the military bases of the Expressionist revolt. In the cafés of Berlin, Munich, Dresden, Leipzig, Darmstadt, Prague, Vienna, Zurich, Hannover, and elsewhere these young Germans came together, discovered and nurtured a mutual desire for changing the contemporary world and worked out common solutions. In this way they provided their movement with its basic organization and momentum.

The café was immortalized in numerous Expressionist poems. One of the finest examples is Iwan Goll's "Café," originally published in April, 1914 in *Die Aktion*. Goll stresses the sincerity of friendships, the naturalness of character and the importance of conversation (lines 11-12) that he found in the café, surrounded by the noisy unfriendliness of the metropolis outside:

> Alle Mitmenschen der Stadt
> Waren nur staubige, blasse Laternen,

Wuchernd mit fremdem Licht. —
Nur hier fand ich Freunde,
Echte Wälder noch, verdornt und tief,
Oder Ebenen
Mit windreinem Fühlen.
Hier war Instinkt von schönen Tieren,
Hände hatten die Geste
Von knospenden Rosen.

Wie Musik
Schwebte, was sie sprachen,
Über dem Rauschen der Cyklopenstadt.[81]

All my fellow men of the city
Were only dusty, pale lanterns,
Teeming with alien light. —
Only here did I find friends,
Natural forests still, bethorned and deep,
Or plains
With wind-pure senses.
Here was the instinct of noble animals,
Hands had the gesture
Of blossoming roses.

Like music,
What they said hovered
Above the roar of the cyclopean city.

VI   *The Life and Death of the Movement*

Clearly implicit in the revolutionary movement represented in
Lotz's "Jugend" cycle was a development through discernible
stages; this, too, like so much else in that work, mirrors (and antici-
pates) the actual course of events in Expressionism as a whole.
There were three distinct phases in the movement, all of them con-
ditioned in large part by prominent political developments in the
era.

The first phase (1910–14) was the period of the founding and ex-
pansion of the movement. It coincided with the years in which the
atmosphere of political crisis was intensified to the extreme, until it
exploded into war during the summer of 1914. At the beginning of
this phase, as Rudolf Kayser described it in an early (1918) history
of the movement, the Expressionists went underground into the

smoke-filled backrooms of the artist cafés.[82] Their central concerns in these years were largely human, spiritual, moral, or social issues. They directed their major efforts at investigating and then healing the wounds inflicted on the psychic life of man by a repressive and corruptive society. Only in isolated instances — most notably in the circle of writers and thinkers around Pfemfert's *Die Aktion* — was there a noticeable interest in concrete political issues and in changing the structure of Wilhelminian government. The representative poetry of this phase is thus that which deals with the subjective life of man, especially the sensitive, thinking man of the big city: e.g., the poems in the collections edited by Hiller *(Der Kondor,* 1912) and Meyer *(Der Mistral — The Mistral,* 1913), or the important volumes of verse by Blass *(Die Strassen komme ich entlang geweht — I Come Drifting Down the Streets,* 1912) and Stadler *(Der Aufbruch — Breaking Away,* 1912). Just as the movement reached a high-point of excitement and support in 1913-14, the First World War broke out, launching the second phase.

Not surprisingly, the major issue of this phase (1914-18) was the Great War. Many Expressionists looked upon the war initially — for the most part because of their political indifference (and ignorance) up to that time — as a "liberation from middle-class narrowness and pettiness...from all of what is felt to be — either consciously or unconsciously — the satiation, the stifling atmosphere and the fossilization of our world...."[83] Having been inducted into military service, or having volunteered in their exuberance over a seeming "liberation," the great majority went off to war in its first year. Very soon, once they were confronted with the ugly and horrifying realities of modern warfare and discovered that this would be no six-month campaign like that of 1870-71, they began to turn against the conflagration and see it as a concrete sign of all that was politically wrong with their world. The frightening and dehumanizing images of battle began to obsess their minds; they recorded the horrors and the suffering of it in their writings. The representative poem of this phase is the war poem. Prominent examples of it, written by soldier-poets, such as Wilhelm Klemm, Oskar Kanehl, Alfred Lichtenstein, Walter Ferl, and Erwin Piscator, appeared throughout the war in a series which was published in *Die Aktion* under the rubric "Verse vom Schlachtfeld" ("Verses from the Battlefield," 1914-18).

The final phase (1918-24) was opened by the November Revolution in 1918, which ended the 1000-year-old rule of monarchies in

Germany and Austria and erected in their place, for the first time in German or Austrian history, a democratic republic. In overwhelming numbers the Expressionists, seasoned politically by the fires of war, threw their full support behind the revolution at its very outset. They conceived of it as the culmination of a decade of struggling, as the realization of their original fight to change their world internally, guided now by the rude awakening to the harsh external political realities they had just experienced. The many poems which hail the revolution or offer it political programs in the anthology edited by Rubiner in the spring of 1919 *(Kameraden der Menschheit)* are representative of the dominant poetry of this period.

Much puzzled thought has been devoted by scholars to discovering the reasons for the demise of Expressionism as a movement in the early 1920s. The causes remain unclear, obscured in most part by the confusion of events on almost all levels of human activity in what were for Germany extremely troubled and often chaotic years. There is no point in listing here all the possible reasons offered in the voluminous scholarly literature. However, the factors which stand out as especially significant are perhaps worth mentioning.

Most Expressionists who had supported the November Revolution felt betrayed once they saw control over the new government pass into the hands of the more moderate, middle-of-the-road parties. The left wing, socialist, and communist parties which they had followed were forced to assume an at most peripheral role in the shaky republic. Thus, in disappointment, sometimes even in bitter withdrawal, they turned their backs on the Revolution, and with it on the movement that had led them to it.

Also, while the Expressionists waged a hard-fought battle against tremendous opposition to assert their ideas and make themselves heard and read in the prewar years, by 1919-20 Expressionism had become the dominant tendency, the established art. The hard fight, which always tends to consolidate and solidify supporters and movements, had been won. There was no longer the urgent need for concerted efforts. The Expressionists were widely accepted by the general public. Having achieved a measure or more of success, they, of course, were inclined to go on to new experiences and new experiments — to new movements, new aesthetics, and new philosophies. Thus the movement seemed to break up almost naturally of its own account.

CHAPTER 5

Styles

THE plurals in this and the next chapter headings have a special significance in the scholarly literature on Expressionism. Since the 1920s, when scholars made their first serious attempts to come to terms with Expressionist literature, it has been readily assumed that its thematic scope was large. And yet — in retrospect this now seems odd — the concept of an equivalent stylistic plurality was staunchly resisted. It was as though one single, new style had to be found in all texts if the term "Expressionism" was to have any real validity as a period concept. But the search for such a style has apparently been abandoned in recent years.[1] It was, of course, an approach predicated from the start on a shaky foundation. The number of authors and the volume of literature involved strongly militated against the possibility of any one style. Moreover, the force and impact of the events taking place between 1910 and 1919 were too powerful to be shrugged off by the Expressionists and too overwhelming for them to adhere to any simple kind of uniformity, in any area of endeavor, for a significant span of time. A stylistic analysis of this literature that takes both the history of the movement and the development of its individual representatives into account yields an eclectic complex of various techniques instead of a rigid, homogeneous system. In fact, we can really only discuss style in terms of general tendencies that are not necessarily characteristic of any single author or any single stage of the movement.

The main concerns of the Expressionists were ideological, after all, and not aesthetic. That was the whole point of their outspoken opposition to "l'art pour l'art" and their programmatic stress on ethical commitment. Stylistically, almost anything is possible in this literature; it ranges over the whole linguistic spectrum.[2] It can be, in one instance, radically experimental; in another, very "classical"; and, in still another, colloquial or pedestrian. Even regional dialect is possible.[3] And all of these stylistic levels can be inter-mingled in the same text; "dictional purity" is not a category in Ex-pressionism. The main criterion for the Expressionist poet in se-lecting any stylistic mode is clearly not an extraneous standard, but whether it can serve as an appropriate and meaningful superstruc-ture for the sense and sentiments inherent in the content. This is, of course, the most fitting counterpart to the relativism, the openness, the universality of the world view espoused by the movement. Only in this sense can Expressionism be considered a stylistic revolution as well as an ideological one: it was a liberation of poetic expression from prescribed forms.

I   *The Disrupted Perspective*

A good deal, perhaps even the bulk, of Expressionist poetry is formally quite conventional. We can cite as a representative samp-ling *Menschheitsdämmerung* (1919-20), the most important anth-ology of Expressionist poetry, spanning the whole decade before its appearance. A substantial number of the poems in it make use of conventional line, syntactic, and stanzaic structure. A famous poem from the first section of that volume, Lichtenstein's "Die Däm-merung" ("Twilight," 1911), will illustrate the point:

> Ein dicker Junge spielt mit einem Teich.
> Der Wind hat sich in einem Baum gefangen.
> Der Himmel sieht verbummelt aus und bleich,
> Als wäre ihm die Schminke ausgegangen.
>
> Auf lange Krücken schief herabgebückt
> Und schwatzend kriechen auf dem Feld zwei Lahme.
> Ein blonder Dichter wird vielleicht verrückt.
> Ein Pferdchen stolpert über eine Dame.
>
> An einem Fenster klebt ein fetter Mann.
> Ein Jüngling will ein weiches Weib besuchen.
> Ein grauer Clown zieht sich die Stiefel an.
> Ein Kinderwagen schreit und Hunde fluchen.[4]
>
> A fat boy is playing with a pond.
> The wind has gotten caught in a tree.

> The sky looks dissolute and pale,
> As though it had run out of make-up.
>
> Bent crooked on long crutches
> And chattering, two cripples are creeping across the field.
> A blond poet is perhaps going mad.
> A pony trips over a lady.
>
> A fat man is sticking to a window.
> A young lad wants to visit a supple woman.
> A gray clown is putting on his boots.
> A baby carriage screams and dogs are cursing.

Both in form and content the poem was unmistakably inspired by Hoddis's "Weltende."[5] It borrows from its model the traditional alternating rhyme scheme (abab), meter (iambic), stanzaic structure (four line), line length (pentameter) and syntax (parataxis with standard grammar). Nonetheless, the poem still strikes the reader as being odd, somehow unsettling, even perhaps as being the product of a disturbed or lunatic mind. On the one hand, there is a clear undercurrent of humor in such phrases as "A fat boy is playing with a pond," "The sky looks dissolute and pale/As though it had run out of make-up" and "A fat man is sticking to a window." Yet, the title of the poem seems best suited for a serious theme. This tone is struck also by such potentially grave lines as "A blond poet is perhaps going mad," "A gray clown is putting on his boots" and "A baby carriage screams and dogs are cursing."

It is, in fact, the very mixture of the grave and the ludicrous in this poem which accounts in great part for the sense of disorientation and the grotesqueness of vision that inform it so strongly. The perspective established through the imagery of the poem reinforces this impression. The mere choice of words is crucial here: they are consistently inappropriate by normal standards. A boy, for example, does not normally play "with" a pond, but, of course, "in" it; the wind usually does not "get caught" in trees; the sky cannot, as a rule, be described as "dissolute," or be thought of as wearing "make-up". What the poet accomplishes by couching what are essentially common words in a highly incongruous context is to upset or reverse conventional ("consensus") perspective. In other words, he disrupts the established space relationship of things and people, so that subject becomes object and object, subject.[6] The result is startling: inanimate objects can now assume human qualities; and human figures — no longer superior to external reality, but on an equal footing with it — are capable of acting objectlike ("A fat man is sticking to a window").

The pervading sense of disorientation one feels when reading this poem is further enhanced by the syntax: the predominant parataxis neatly arranges a series of simply structured clauses and sentences whose relationship should then be apparent. However, none of them are causally connected as they conventionally would be (through the use of conjunctions such as "because," "after," "before," etc.)[7] It is left to the puzzled and troubled reader to discover the unifying factor or force at work somewhere beyond the disjointed surface reality.

The overall impact of the poem on the reader is very close to that of "Weltende." Having read through to the end and then reconsidered the title (which now might conjure up both connotations of the German word "Dämmerung": viz., both an end — "dusk" — and a beginning — "dawn" — of a world), the reader feels as if he had paid a visit to a topsy-turvy world in which seemingly harmless or insignificant events — a boy playing in a pond, two cripples crossing a field, a baby crying in a carriage — have assumed ominous implications.

Lichtenstein's ultimate aim in "Die Dämmerung," common to the Expressionist movement as a whole, is to induce his reader to reassess established reality in new terms and consider alternatives. Of course, it might be claimed that all poetry is informed by that purpose. But in Expressionism it is pursued aggressively, with an unsettling determination and a profound moral intent seldom encountered in German verse before 1910.

II   *Unconventional Imagery*

Many Expressionist poets make use of the mixture of tones and disrupted perspective we found in Lichtenstein's and Hoddis's poems. But there are many other, related stylistic devices used in this poetry to satisfy the same politico-aesthetic aim.

Heym was a master of the technique first introduced by the French Symbolists (particularly Charles Baudelaire and Arthur Rimbaud) of using startling or very unusual imagery to awaken the reader's sensibilities.[8] The structure and form of his poems is

largely conventional. With few exceptions, they use iambic penta-
meter in rhymed quatrains and paratactic syntax. This conven-
tionality, however, only serves to intensify, by dramatic contrast
with the content, the unsettling effects of the poem. For Heym's
poems paint frightening, often seemingly hallucinatory pictures of
modern life. They center on realms of experience usually over-
looked or shunned by the Wilhelminian materialist mind, and insist
that their shocked reader respond. In Heym's poetry, inscrutable
yet powerful forces defy standard categories of thought (Kantian
logic) and disintegrate the neat divisions of reality established in
time and space by Western civilization.

Heym's "Ophelia" (1910) is the first of many Expressionist ver-
sions of a Shakespearean motif, most directly inspired by Rim-
baud's 1870 "Ophélie." Even without any embellishment from
Heym's pen, this motif would have appealed to the Expressionists
because of its themes of insanity and suicide. Yet, like his fellow
recusant poets, Heym was not interested in merely recording
history, but in rewriting it. He placed his Ophelia in a distinctly
contemporary setting and then boldly shifted the ideological per-
spective from an Elizabethan to a post-Nietzschean vantage point.
A pack of water rats nesting in her hair, Ophelia floats down the
river (into which she has cast herself), "through the shadow of the
primordial forest that rests in the water," on past the transient din
and drone of the towering cities of the modern world, disappearing
finally into the "eternities" of the biological cycle of life:

> Der Strom trägt weit sie fort, die untertaucht,
> Durch manchen Winters trauervollen Port.
> Die Zeit hinab. Durch Ewigkeiten fort,
> Davon der Horizont wie Feuer raucht.[9]

> She submerges, as the stream carries her forth afar,
> Through the mournful ports of many winters.
> Down through time. Forth through eternities,
> Which smoke like fires on the horizon.

The seemingly solid foundations of civilization (represented by the
great cities in which contemporary man has placed his faith and
energies) thus begin to slip away, as Heym finally installs the only
absolutes of life, not in a biblically documented higher sphere, not
in material and technological progress, but in the fluid intangibili-

ties of the eternal recurrence of earthly existence. It was a startling vision for the Wilhelminian reader who lacked Heym's schooling in Nietzsche.

Similar doubt is cast on the basis of contemporary urban life in Heym's "Der Gott der Stadt" ("The God of the City," 1910). Here the potential inherent in the modern, industrial metropolis for turning against itself through excessive growth is personified in the god of the new cities, who is not a benevolent shelterer of man, but a frightening, angry, fire-belching, primitive idol (Baal) who sits atop the sprawling blocks of houses and consumes the streets with his hot flames:

> Auf einem Häuserblocke sitzt er breit.
> Die Winde lagern schwarz um seine Stirn.
> Er schaut voll Wut, wo fern in Einsamkeit
> Die letzten Häuser in das Land verirrn.
>
> . . .
>
> Er streckt ins Dunkel seine Fleischerfaust.
> Er schüttelt sie. Ein Meer von Feuer jagt
> Durch eine Strasse. Und der Glutqualm braust
> Und frisst sie auf, bis spät der Morgen tagt.[10]
>
> On a block of houses he spreads his weight.
> The winds rest blackly round his brow.
> He looks with rage into the distant solitude,
> Where the last houses are lost in the land.
>
> . . .
>
> He stretches out his butcher's fist into the gloom.
> He shakes it. A sea of fire surges
> Through a street. And the smoke and fire roars
> And devours it, till day breaks late.

III *The Absolute Metaphor*

Another technique practiced by many Expressionist poets to stir the reader's sensibilities profoundly also derived from French Symbolism, specifically this time from Rimbaud's unique use of metaphor. Traditionally, the associations of a metaphor had been established in a poem by direct juxtaposition or comparison. This practice allowed the reader to move comfortably through each line and image of the poem to its end. Since the import of the poem had become apparent by the time he had reached the last line, he felt no compulsion to systematically reassess its totality. However, in Rimbaud's work (most notably his famous "Bateau ivre" of 1871) and then in the work of his many German Expressionist followers (Trakl, Benn, Stramm, Ehrenstein, Goll, et al.), words were used metaphorically in almost complete isolation and without any apparent associative context (the "alogical" or "absolute metaphor"). Such metaphors act as oblique fragments of the poet's total sensibility, which treats the things of reality directly, i.e., without the obvious intervention of consciousness.[11] It is only in the total context of the poem that the chaos of the poet's images begins to assume clearer meaning. Since it is the reader's mind that must, in the end, achieve the synthesis of all these disparate images, he has to become much more intimately and actively involved in the poetic process in this kind of poetry than in more conventional verse. He must rethink the images of the poem at each stage of its development and then its totality at the conclusion, when he is forced to return to the very beginning in the title and start responding to it once more.

This technique is already inherent in Hoddis's and Lichtenstein's use of asyndetic, paratactic lines, which have no clear connection with one another except that which is implied by the entire poem. The "absolute metaphor" generally communicates with the reader even more subtly and cryptically, since it is most often expressed in only one or two of the words most essential to it; qualifying words (especially articles, adjectives, and adverbs) are generally excluded. The resultant extreme brevity of the language in such verse greatly enhances the allusive values of the individual words. Trakl's "Ruh und Schweigen" ("Peace and Silence," 1913) is one of the finest poems in this style:

Hirten begruben die Sonne im kahlen Wald.
Ein Fischer zog
In härenem Netz den Mond aus frierendem Weiher.

In blauem Kristall
Wohnt der bleiche Mensch, die Wang' an seine Sterne gelehnt;
Oder er neigt das Haupt in purpurnem Schlaf.

Doch immer rührt der schwarze Flug der Vögel
Den Schauenden, das Heilige blauer Blumen,
Denkt die nahe Stille Vergessenes, erloschene Engel.

Wieder nachtet die Stirne in mondenem Gestein;
Ein strahlender Jüngling
Erscheint die Schwester in Herbst und schwarzer Verwesung.[12]

Shepherds buried the sun in barren woods.
A fisherman pulled
The moon in hempen net from icy pond.

In blue crystal
Dwells the pallid man, his cheek resting on his stars;
Or he lowers his head in purple sleep.

Yet always the black flight of birds touches
The beholder, the sacredness of blue flowers,
The close stillness contemplates things forgotten, extinguished angels.

Again his brow darkens in moon rocks;
A radiant youth
His sister appears in autumn and black decay.

The individual images of this poem are annoyingly abstruse when
considered separately: "Shepherds buried the sun in barren
woods," "A fisherman pulled/The moon in hempen net from icy
pond," "In blue crystal/Dwells the pallid man." Yet as we reach
the end of the poem, the very last word ("decay") clearly suggests
the basic theme of death. Indeed, if we return to the title and begin
to reread the poem, we sense that it is an attempt to transvalue the
conventional meaning of death. Death here is not the painful end
of life that it is traditionally; rather, it is conceived of as a har-
monious part of existence which evokes feelings of "peace and si-
lence." There is no sense of loss or separation, but instead of re-
union and completion: man returns in death to his true origins in
the elements. All divisions in space (lines 1-3, 5) and time (lines 11-
12) are obliterated, and man once more has a sense of peaceful one-
ness with the universe (lines 4-8, 12). The divisive force in man,
consciousness, which (through the cognitive norms of time and
space) had separated him from his natural surroundings, has been
extinguished. This latter fact is alluded to in two sets of images: the
metaphors for the burial of the sun (traditionally associated with

Apollo, reason, consciousness) and the raising of the moon (traditionally associated with feeling, passion, dreams, the unconscious); and the references to "stillness" contemplating "things forgotten" (i.e., the absence of memory), "extinguished angels" (i.e., conceptualized religion, something posited by man's mind in external reality) and the "darkening" of man's brow. Death is here no more than a natural part of the cycle of life ("decay"), but no less also than the sole absolute of existence (the angels, an extension of God, are "extinguished" in death). Thus, the crisis-ridden and divided world in which Trakl was writing in 1913 was transformed by his poetic vision into a harmonious totality.[13]

IV *The Development of the Concentrated Style*

Trakl's use of the absolute metaphor leads almost inevitably to a compression of language and to a loosening up of traditional poetic structure. Single words are used in isolation without any qualifiers or connectives. The metrical structure centers on an almost self-determined pattern of stressed syllables, rather than on a symmetrical alternation of accented and unaccented ones. (With articles and qualifying adjectives, along with their endings, reduced to a bare minimum, such symmetry is almost impossible). Rhyme is not easily achieved in this kind of verse; the poet often feels that it inhibits expression. Thus the metrical structure of "Ruh und Schweigen," as of most of Trakl's poetry, is very irregular (an uneven mixture of iambs and dactyls). The rhythm and symmetry are established not by meter and rhyme, but by the more "primitive"[14] system of parallelisms (in Trakl's poem, the rhythmic alternation of short and long lines in stanzas one, two, and four, and the succession of lines of gradually increasing length in stanza three) and of assonance and alliteration. The key vowels throughout "Ruh und Schweigen" are "a," "o," "u"; they are deep, back vowels, which are appropriate to the theme of peace in death and which allude phonically to the first word in the title. The main alliterating consonant is "s"; it occurs in variation in every line and is especially prominent in key words in each line; it points phonically to the second noun in the title.

The concentration of language and freedom of rhythmic structure became more and more prominent and extreme in Expressionist literature (poetry, prose, and drama) as the movement gained momentum, especially after 1914. Since it was a later development, it was well-remembered by Expressionists and critics alike. The result was that hyper-concentrated and syntactically and grammatically distorted language (often called the "telegram style," because it resembles the choppy, staccato phrases in a telegram message) eventually — and wrongly — became exclusively associated in the public mind with the notion of an "Expressionist style."[15]

There were two major foreign influences on this development in Germany. Walt Whitman, whose poetry was widely read and discussed (and even translated) by the Expressionists, provided a convincing model for liberating rhythmic structure in poetry.[16] His long, free flowing, unrhymed lines are noticeably reflected in poems by Werfel, Becher, Stadler, Rubiner, Goll (especially in the 1918 version of his long poem "Der Panama-Kanal" — "The Panama Canal"), Otten and others. The second important foreign influence here came not from a poetic model, but from a loudly espoused poetic theory, contained in the Futurist manifestoes of the Italian iconoclast and brainstorming theoretician-poet F. T. Marinetti (first published in German translation in the spring of 1912 in *Der Sturm*).[17] In his controversial formulae for a new poetic style, Marinetti enumerated, among other things: the destruction of syntax, by arranging substantives in the arbitrary order dictated by inspiration ("One must destroy syntax and scatter one's nouns at random just as they are born"[18]); the predominant use of the noun over other parts of speech, with a special preference for the compound (and particularly the hyphenated noun); the use of verbs in the infinitive, so that they will better "adapt themselves" to the nouns; and the abolition of adjectives, adverbs, and conventional punctuation. Marinetti believed that the adoption of this program would free language from ossified and restricting traditions and enable it to express the new, accelerated tempo and aggressive tone of life in the modern cities.

Marinetti's ideas were much publicized and given unusually wide critical coverage in the contemporary German press, largely because of the brash publicity tactics he used during his noisy visits to Berlin (spring, 1912; February and November, 1913). He was therefore able to lend weighty support to many of the ideological tendencies in Expressionism which I have discussed in this study (e.g., the opposition to cultural and artistic passivity, the revolt against the past, the removal of the restrictions of time and space on artistic expression, the intense interest in life in the modern metropolis). And he also left an unmistakable imprint on Expressionist poetic practice, most conspicuously by conceptualizing, and thereby accelerating after about the middle of the early phase of the movement, the already detectable Expressionist tendency to reduce poetic language to its skeletal essentials and to subvert the standard rules of grammar and syntax.[19]

Broadly speaking, we can distinguish two schools in this particular development in Expressionist poetry: a conservative one and a highly radical one. To follow the gradual progression of this tendency side by side with the development of Expressionism we will have to leave Trakl, who died at the very outset of the war (November, 1914), and turn to a poet whose career spans the whole decade. Benn's work between about 1912 and the end of the Expressionist era represents the first of the two schools just mentioned.

One of Benn's early poems, "Nachtcafé" ("Night Café," 1912), already carries this kind of concentration of language a full degree further than Trakl did, although it is still at a very moderate stage here. The concentration in this particular poem, as in many others written by Benn in this period, derives from a form of personification which Expressionist literature often employs to disrupt normal perspective. The poet's vision zeroes in on isolated aspects of his poetic subjects and then, lending them human attributes, he has them stand for the whole (synecdoche). We encountered some limited use of this kind of personification in Lichtenstein's "Die Dämmerung" (lines 2-4, 12), where it complemented the other disorienting effects of the poem. But Benn's more consistent use of it ruthlessly draws the reader's attention again and again to basic — even "ugly" — physical undercurrents of life, as they are discovered here in the contacts which men and women make in a café. The poem begins:

824: Der Frauen Liebe und Leben.
Das Cello trinkt rasch mal. Die Flöte
rülpst tief drei Takte lang: das schöne Abendbrot.
Die Trommel liest den Kriminalroman zu Ende.

Grüne Zähne, Pickel im Gesicht
winkt einer Lidrandentzündung.

Fett im Haar
spricht zu offenem Mund mit Rachenmandel
Glaube Liebe Hoffnung um den Hals.[20]

824: the loves and lives of women.
The cello takes a quick drink. The flute
belches three bass beats long: his pleasant evening meal.
The drum gets finished with his detective novel.

Green teeth, pimples on his face
waves to a conjunctivitis.

Grease in hair
talks to open mouth with tonsils
Faith Hope Charity round his neck.

The language becomes even more concise (reduced at first to little more than a list of nouns), as Benn makes his basic point more clearly in describing the entrance of a tan-skinned woman followed by a fleshy fat man. She is a haunting symbol of the true, primitive ("Desert dried out. Canaanite brown") essence of life, which is not — as the contemporary Wilhelminian perspective would have it — cerebral (see lines 4–5 below), but profoundly sensual:

Die Tür fliesst hin: Ein Weib.
Wüste ausgedorrt. Kanaanitisch braun.
Keusch. Höhlenreich. Ein Duft kommt mit. Kaum Duft.
Es ist nur eine süsse Verwölbung der Luft
gegen mein Gehirn.

Eine Fettleibigkeit trippelt hinterher.

The door wafts open: A Woman.
Desert dried out. Canaanite brown.
Chaste. Cavernous. A fragrance follows. Scarcely fragrance.
It is only a sweet swelling of the air
against my brain.

Fatfleshiness trips along behind.

A more famous poem by Benn, with a closely related theme, is "D-Zug" ("Express Train," 1912). Written shortly after "Nachtcafé," "D-Zug" utilizes a far more concentrated language. It also introduces into his work the conspicuous use of the kind of compound substantives (often hyphenated) that were advocated by Marinetti; they function by themselves here, as elsewhere in Benn's work, as absolute metaphors. The poem opens with two lines, lacking verbs and most qualifiers, in which the allusion to man's sensual (here especially sexual) essence is pared down to the mere notation of colors and the allusion to the destination of a train ride:

> Braun wie Kognak. Braun wie Laub. Rotbraun. Malaiengelb.
> D-Zug Berlin-Trelleborg und die Ostseebäder.
>
> Fleisch, das nackt ging.
> Bis in den Mund gebräunt vom Meer.
> Reif gesenkt, zu griechischem Glück.
> In Sichel-Sehnsucht: wie weit der Sommer ist!
> Vorletzter Tag des neunten Monats schon!
>
> Stoppel und letzte Mandel lechzt in uns.
> Entfaltungen, das Blut, die Müdigkeiten,
> die Georginennähe macht uns wirr.
>
> Männerbraun stürzt sich auf Frauenbraun:
>
> Eine Frau ist etwas für eine Nacht.
> Und wenn es schön war, noch für die nächste!
> Oh! Und dann wieder dies Bei-sich-selbst-Sein!
> Diese Stummheiten! Dies Getriebenwerden!
>
> Eine Frau ist etwas mit Geruch.
> Unsägliches! Stirb hin! Resede.
> Darin ist Süden, Hirt und Meer.
> An jedem Abhang lehnt ein Glück.
>
> Frauenhellbraun taumelt an Männerdunkelbraun:
>
> Halte mich! Du, ich falle!
> Ich bin im Nacken so müde.
> Oh, dieser fiebernde süsse
> letzte Geruch aus den Gärten.[21]
>
> Brown like cognac. Brown like leaves. Red-brown.
>   Malayan yellow.
> Express train Berlin-Trelleborg and the Baltic Sea resorts.
>
> Flesh that walked naked.
> Browned to the lips by the sea.
> Lowered ripe, to Greek bliss.
> In sickle-desire: How far the summer is!
> Just two more days of the ninth month left!

Stubble and last amygdala yearns in us.
Unfoldings, the blood, the weariness,
the nearness of dahlias addles our minds.
Man-brown falls upon woman-brown:

A woman is something for a night.
And if it was nice, for the next one, too!
Oh! And then this being-by-oneself again!
These silences! This being-driven!

A woman is something with odor.
Ineffable! Expire! Reseda.
Therein is the South, shepherd and sea.
On every slope reclines a joy.

Woman-bright-brown reels against man-dark-brown:

Hold me! My love, I'm falling!
My neck is so tired.
Oh, this delirious sweet
last smell from the gardens.

Finally, a poem from Benn's later Expressionist phase, "Der Sänger" ("The Singer," 1925), will illustrate the furthest point reached by this development in his work. The poem is the first of several written by Benn during his long poetic career on the traditional theme of the Orphic singer: the poet as journeyer into the unseen depths and as magical charmer. In Benn's poem, the Thracian singer has become the Expressionist reformer who can mend through his song the division in man's psyche fostered by the excesses of the post-Enlightenment mind. It begins with a series of metaphoric nouns:

Keime, Begriffsgenesen,
Broadways, Azimut,
Turf- und Nebelwesen
mischt der Sänger im Blut,
immer in Gestaltung,
immer dem Worte zu
nach Vergessen der Spaltung
zwischen ich und du.[22]

> Seed-buds, geneses of concepts,
> Broadways, azimuth,
> creatures of turf and mist
> the singer mixes in his blood,
> always shaping,
> always towards the word
> towards forgetting the split
> between I and Thou.

V *The Theory and Practice of "Wortkunst"*

The radical school of poets carried the concentrated style to its ultimate extreme; it was almost as though these poets wanted to observe Marinetti's formulae to the letter. Most representatives of this tendency were closely associated with the circle around *Der Sturm,* which had sponsored Marinetti's visits to Berlin as well as the coincidental exhibitions of Futurist art in the *Sturm* galleries. Walden's circle embraced Marinetti's program wholeheartedly, and then reformulated and elaborated on it in a series of essays published in *Der Sturm* during the war (1915-18), eventually renaming it "Wortkunst" ("word art").[23]

The "Wortkunst" theory is the clearest formulation of the basic Expressionist ethic in almost purely aesthetic terms. In practice, the ultimate aim of this elaborate theory was to help to reestablish in the reader the sense of oneness with the universe which he had enjoyed before the logical mind achieved primacy after the Enlightenment. In conventional poetry, the omnipresence of the logical faculty is evidenced most clearly in the insistence on established grammar and a systematically developed and representationally depicted content. Such poetry communicates with the reader on the whole indirectly, for example, by means of straightforward descriptions of the things observed or through analogies (logical comparisons formed by prepositions, such as "like" or "as"). The "Wortkunst" attempts to communicate more directly by presenting images to the reader which act not as substitutes for the essential reality of existence ("the spiritual reality"), but as that very reality in themselves. The principal structural means for achieving this is by shifting the emphasis in a poem from that traditionally placed on the meanings of words to one placed on rhythm and the sound values of words. This shift is accomplished through what one "Wortkunst" theorist terms "concentration" and "decentration."[24]
"Concentration" is the reduction of language to its barest essen-

tials; "decentration," the substitution of word repetition, parallel-isms, word associations, and inversions for traditional meter and rhyme. The overall unifying elements in this poetry are the central images and the rhythm, not the established meanings of words and metrical structure. We have already encountered both of these principles at work in earlier Expressionist poetry, of course. The difference in "Wortkunst" poetry is that they are taken more literally and practiced much more consistently.

The leading practitioner and the great model for the advocates of this style in the *Sturm* circle was Stramm. His poems began to appear there in April, 1914, shortly after his first meeting with its editor. He very soon attracted a large following of imitators, whose work filled the pages of the journal alongside his; they included Rudolf Blümner, Lothar Schreyer, Kurt Liebmann, Otto Nebel, and Franz Richard Behrens.[25].

Stramm's "Trieb" ("Urge"), an early poem which first appeared in the December, 1914 issue of *Der Sturm,* is a typical and very effective example of the "Wortkunst" theory in practice:

> Schrecken Sträuben
> Wehren Ringen
> Ächzen Schluchzen
> Stürzen
> Du!
> Grellen Gehren
> Winden Klammern
> Hitzen Schwächen
> Ich und Du!
> Lösen Gleiten
> Stöhnen Wellen
> Schwinden Finden
> Ich
> Dich
> Du![26]

> Startling struggling
> Resisting wrestling
> Groaning sobbing
> Tumbling
> Thou!
> Shrilling questing
> Twisting clinging
> Heating weakening

> I and Thou!
> Loosening sliding
> Moaning waving
> Fading finding
> I
> Thee
> Thou!

The poem consists of only nineteen gerunds, six pronouns, and one connecting word; all qualifiers have been eliminated. "Grellen" and "Gehren" could theoretically be plural forms of the feminine weak nouns "Grelle" ("piercing sharpness of sound/glaring brightness of color") and "Gehre" ("harpoon"). But it is evidence of the strength of the rhythmic structure that, in the proximity of the dominant forms, we tend to assimilate these words to the others and read them as verbal nouns, too, coined by the poet from the adjective "grell" ("shrill") and the verb "begehren" ("to desire"). Each of the nineteen nouns is highly suggestive of intense, vigorous, or violent physical action. That this action is executed not by a single individual, but in an intimate relationship between two individuals, is implied by several of the nouns ("Schrecken," "Sträuben," "Wehren," "Ringen," "Klammern," "Lösen," "Finden"), when they are read in the context of the familiar singular pronoun "Du" (line 5) and the juxtaposed pronouns "Du" and "Ich" (lines 13-15, 19), which appear at crucial points.

If we place the allusions to physical activity and intimacy in the context alluded to by the title, then the poem can be interpreted as a representation of the acting out of the sexual urge; it is a representation of sexual intercourse through the stages of embrace and penetration (lines 1-5), orgasm (lines 6-9), and relaxation and withdrawal (lines 10-15). The emotional power of the poem derives in large part from the totally subjective perspective of the poet. There is no external description of action, only a recording of the sensations and thoughts experienced in intercourse.

The powerful rhythmic structure of the poem enhances this perspective and the theme. It is established initially by the parallel series of nouns in lines 1-3 (each line with four syllables, alternately stressed and unstressed), which begin a sentence closed by three syllables (stressed-unstressed-stressed) spread over two lines (4-5). This structure is duplicated over the next four lines, with the three closing syllables arranged this time (to underscore the content) within one line. The final six lines repeat this structure once more, the last three syllables now constituting separate lines and all of them stressed, effectively marking the close of the poem. The syllabic parallelisms are further supported by the assonance and alliterations which set off the noun pairs. The alliteration, with the help of the pronoun "Du," also distinguishes stanzaic structure: stanza one (lines 1-5), alliteration of "r," "s," "z"; stanza two (lines 6-9), alliteration of "g," "l"; stanza three (lines 10-15), alliteration of "l," "s," "t."

For a "Wortkunst" poem to have meaning, we must be able to respond to its sounds. A deeper analysis of individual words or phrases would only lead the reader astray, since qualifiers and the clarifying structure of grammar are absent. Language in the usual sense of written or spoken symbols, whose specific reference to objects or ideas is fixed by traditional usage, is scarcely present. The "Wortkunst" poem is composed out of standard vocabulary as far removed as possible from the restricting burdens of a cultural tradition which the Expressionists were attempting to overthrow both artistically and ideologically. Any further step in this direction would mean the total destruction of language and the substitution for it of a completely new, abstract system of sounds. It would be the closest equivalent of the total abstractionism in art, which many Expressionist painters had been practicing since Wassily Kandinsky painted the first abstract canvas in 1910. The equivalent in poetry was dubbed "absolute Dichtung" ("absolute poetry") by Blümner shortly after the war.[27] The first experiments with absolute poetry were executed in Zurich in 1916 in Dadaism, an offshoot most directly of the iconoclastic and antilogical tendencies in Expressionism. The leader of Zurich Dada was the poet Hugo Ball, who created with what he called his "Lautgedichte" ("sound poems") the first totally abstract poems.[28]

Ball's aim in these poems, as he explained in the first Dada manifesto (read in the "Cabaret Voltaire" on July 14, 1916), was to reestablish the primacy of the word by ridding poetry of "all the filth that clings to this accursed language."[29] He was seeking a way back to the "innermost alchemy of the word" by renouncing "the language that journalism has abused and corrupted."[30] In other words, Ball wanted to liberate man's intellectual and emotional sensibilities through a concomitant liberation of the word, to which man's sensibilities are normally bound in social intercourse. Thus, the only syllables we actually recognize in a "sound poem," as in

Ball's most famous one, "Karawane" ("Caravan"), are found in the title alone:

Karawane

> jolifanto bambla o falli bambla
> grossgiga m'pfa habla horem
> egiga goramen
> higo bloiko russula huju
> hollaka hollala
> anlogo bung
> blago bung blago bung
> bosso fataka
> ü üü ü
> schampa wulla wussa olobo
> hej tatta gorem
> eschige zunbada
> wulubu ssubudu uluwu ssubudu
> tumba ba-umf
> kusa gauma
> ba-umf[31]

This is virtually pure sound and pure rhythm. The only associations we might tie in with these syllables are stimulated by the title and the profusion of long, back vowels: we might think of a caravan passing through native villages in the African jungles. But such associations are at best vague and intangible.

Ball had very few followers in this experiment (besides Blümner, they included most notably Nebel, Kurt Schwitters, Richard Huelsenbeck, and Hans Arp). And for Ball, as for most of his followers, it represented a very brief stage in his overall development as a poet. Also, in the body of Expressionist poetry, in striking contrast to Expressionist painting, absolute abstraction of content constitutes an extremely small portion of the total. Nonetheless, the validity of the Ball experiment would seem to have found some proof in its recent revival in the international "Concrete Poetry" movement.[32]

CHAPTER 6

Themes

SINCE the Expressionist rejects any division of art and life, his intimate involvement in his contemporary world, discussed in detail in Chapter 4, quite naturally informs the content of his poetry. Thus, the thematic structure of the general body of Expressionist poetry is conditioned by the specific critical response of the poet to his world as a concrete social, political, and economic reality. We can distinguish in this sense five basic thematic complexes, according to the level on which the poet reacts to this reality and the alternative he proposes: the new reality/anti-Wilhelminian reality; the new morality/anti-Wilhelminian morality; the new politics/anti-Wilhelminian politics; the new vision/anti-Wilhelminian world view; the new man/anti-Wilhelminian man. There is, of course, considerable overlapping of any one complex of themes with one or more of the remaining four. Literature, especially a whole body of it, is obviously much too complex to permit itself to be categorized or catalogued in simplistic terms. Also, a given poem will often involve more than one basic theme or group of themes. What I wish to do here is merely to suggest a framework which will help the new reader to recognize more clearly the thematic cohesiveness of the movement.

I   *The New Reality/Anti-Wilhelminian Reality*

As we have seen, the Expressionist poet dropped out of his contemporary society because of its restricting emphasis on order, discipline, regimentation, and a special deference to authority. He was confronted with these features of society most tangibly in the undemocratic political structure of the Wilhelminian monarchy, the leading role played in the whole society by the military, the monopolistic control over the economy by big industrial concerns, the stifling atmosphere in the schools and the family. He attempted to come to critical terms with this reality in his poetry, to put it behind him and to search out a freer, less rigid, and more fulfilling environment in which to live.

The large number of poems on "Aufbruch" ("breaking away"), "Aufruhr" ("uprising") and "Revolution" in Expressionism are familiar even to those readers who have only a passing acquaintance with the movement. The poems of this sort, particularly those published in the movement's early phase, were seldom inspired by distinctly political motives; rather, they were militant reactions to Wilhelminian Germany on the broadest basis, expressions of a desire to break out of generally oppressive conditions in contemporary existence.

Stadler's "Der Aufbruch" ("Breaking Away," written before 1913) is the most famous of these poems of revolt. Characteristically, Stadler's revolutionary poet is imbued with the qualities of a combatant. This soldier-poet at first retires from the battle, from "reality," into a life of quiet self-indulgence:

> Dann, plötzlich, stand Leben stille. Wege führten
>   zwischen alten Bäumen.
> Gemächer lockten. Es war süss, zu weilen und sich
>   versäumen,
> Von Wirklichkeit den Leib so wie von staubiger
>   Rüstung zu entketten,
> Wollüstig sich in Daunen weicher Traumstunden
>   einzubetten.[1]

> Then, suddenly, life stood still. Paths led between
>   old trees.
> Rooms were enticing. It was sweet to tarry and delay,
> To release the body from reality's chains as though
>   from dusty armor,
> To sleep lustfully in the down of tender hours of dreams.

But then, like a sudden "flashing of lights" in the darkness, he hears the signal which calls him back to the fight:

> Aber eines Morgens rollte durch Nebelluft das Echo
>   von Signalen,
> Hart, scharf, wie Schwerthieb pfeifend. Es war wie wenn
>   im Dunkel plötzlich Lichter aufstrahlen.

Es war wie wenn durch Biwakfrühe Trompetenstösse
   klirren,
   . . .
Ich war in Reihen eingeschient, die in den Morgen stiessen,
   Feuer über Helm und Bügel,
Vorwärts, in Blick und Blut die Schlacht, mit vorge-
   haltenem Zügel.

But one morning the echo of alarms rolled through the
   misty air.
Whistling hard, sharp, like the blow of a sword. It was as
   when lights suddenly flare up in the darkness.
It was as when blasts of trumpets blare in the morning
   through camp,
   . . .
I was locked into the ranks that charged out into the
   morning, fire over helmet and horse,
Forwards, the battle in blood and sight, the reins
   held out in front.

That the poem is about a rebellion against established values and
conditions is suggested perhaps only by the general tone and by
reading it in the context from which it emanated. The enemy is not
clearly identified, but the reward of combat even in defeat — and
this may point to the very motivation for participation as well — is
the passionate pleasure of being able to experience life to its fullest
(something not possible, by implication, in conventional life):

Aber vor dem Erraffen und vor dem Versinken
Würden unsre Augen sich an Welt und Sonne satt und
   glühend trinken.

But before defeat and before we're engulfed
Our eyes would drink their fervent fill of world and sun.

Lotz's "Aufbruch der Jugend" (written before 1914) has been
discussed in a previous context. Lotz also sends his poet into com-
bat, and the reward and motivation in this fight resemble those ex-
pressed in Stadler's poem (see his allusions to the new strength and
vitality which are gained through the revolt). However, whereas
neither the precise nature nor the exact goal of Stadler's battle were
clear, Lotz's "Aufbruch" is obviously directed at an antiquated
and tyrannical monarchy (see the references to "mouldering
crowns" and "infamous prisons").

Becher had a special fondness for the poem of revolution, composing several during the Expressionist era. His most famous, "Ewig im Aufruhr" ("Eternally in Revolt," 1920), parallels Lotz's poem in most details, although Becher's condemnation of the monarchy here, as in most of his other poems of this sort, is much more candid and angry:

> Ewig im Aufruhr
> Wider die Feste
> Wütendster Würger,
> Der Schlächter des Lamms.
> Reisset, zerreisset
> Gewaltsame Böen,
> Finsternisse,
> Den Wucherer-Turm!
> Die Tyrannen
> Zerplatzten auf Thronen.[2]

> Eternally in revolt
> Against the fortress
> Of vilest oppressors,
> The slayers of the lamb.
> Violent squalls,
> Tear, rend
> Shades of evil,
> The usurers' tower!
> The tyrants
> Exploded on thrones.

His earlier, three-part "Päan des Aufruhrs" ("Paean of Revolt," 1913) thrusts the poet into the very leadership of a bloody revolution. The terse grossness of Becher's language is clearly meant to provoke the refined reader:

> Inmitten der Getümmel, knochig und robust,
> Steh ich, befeuernd den Tumult mit Schrei.
> Es schneiden Messer durch die steile Brust,
> Den Acker, hackend Fleisch zu Mampf und Brei.[3]

> Amidst the tumults, strong and robust,
> I stand, firing up the crowds with my cries.
> Knives cut through the towering chest,
> The field, hacking flesh into pulp and paste.

It is a revolution directed against a world, vaguely identifiable in the allusion to the "Reich" ("empire") as Wilhelminian Germany, that is "corrupt to the core" ("bis tief ins Blut verdorben") and that soon lies trampled under the feet of the wrathful revolutionaries:

> Zerstampfet ist des Reiches fade Herrlichkeit.
> Wir Bären heben unsere blanken Eisentatzen.
> An unseren Zähnen kleben Haar und Därme. Speit
> Aus den Frass! Fast unsere Bäuche platzen.

> Trampled is the insipid splendor of the empire.
> We bears raise our sharp iron claws.
> Hair and entrails cling to our teeth. Spit
> Out that slop! Our bellies almost burst.

Becher's revolution is also fired by feelings and ideas identifiable with a desire for an unfettered life:

> Ich wecke dich, verdrängte Kraft! O Anarchie!
> . . .
> Verdammet ewig! Schwerterblitze schwingen,
> Es brechet auf aussätzige Kastenbrust.
> Da schreien Trommeln, alle Türme klingen.
> Hah! Ungestört in nie erträumter Lust!
> . . .
> Verdammet ewig! Eng das Himmelreich,
> Nieder die Tore, wo ihr tretet ein,
> Der Weg verschottert...regenaufgeweicht.
> Hah! Vorwärts marsch in euer Qualdasein!

> I wake you, repressed power! Oh anarchy!
> . . .
> Be damned eternally! Swords swing and clash.
> The leprous chests of castes split open.
> Drums scream; all towers ring.
> Hah! Undisturbed in never-dreamed-of joy!
> . . .
> Be damned eternally! Narrow is the kingdom of heaven,
> Low are the gates, through which you pass;
> The road is bestrewn with stones...softened by rain.
> Hah! Forward march into your tortured existence!

Benn's rejection of the contemporary world in his early volumes of poems *(Morgue und andere Gedichte — Morgue and other poems,* 1912; *Söhne — Sons,* 1913; *Fleisch — Flesh,* 1913) encompassed not only Wilhelminian Germany, but the whole of Western Civilization as well: viz., its myopic disregard of any values and achievements but those based on the empirical sciences, its special respect for the products of cerebral life, its vain idealization of man over other animals. His short poem "Alaska" (1913), for example, begins with the crassly cynical lines:

> Europa, dieser Nasenpopel
> aus einer Konfirmandennase,
> wir wollen nach Alaska gehn.[4]

> Europe, that little glob of filth
> from the nose of a confirmand,
> we want to go to Alaska.

There follows in the next lines a counter-image of man to the conventional ideal that must have made any but the most self-confident middle-class readers of the day bristle with outrage:

> Der Meermensch, der Urwaldmensch,
> der alles aus seinem Bauch gebiert,
> der Robben frisst, der Bären totschlägt,
> der den Weibern manchmal was reinstösst:
> der Mann.

> The man from the sea, the jungle man,
> who bears everything from his belly,
> who gobbles up seals, who kills bears,
> who gives it to his women once in a while:
> the man.

Other Expressionist poetry often directs its critical attention to more specific aspects of contemporary middle-class life. Thus, Arthur Drey in "Die Bürger" ("The Burghers," 1911) and Klabund in "Ein Bürger spricht" ("A Burgher Speaks," 1914) attack the smug materialism of the Wilhelminian citizen.[5] Heym caricatures the stifling narrowness of the contemporary academic world in "Die Professoren" ("The Professors," 1910), while Lichtenstein paints a similar portrait of the life of the omnipresent Wil-helminian bureaucrat in "Der Bureaukrat" (1910).[6] Or there is Becher's summary description of the shallowness, monotony, and narrowness of Wilhelminian family life in "Familie" ("Family," 1912-13). The poem is remarkable for its cold impartiality, yet all the more effective therefore in its criticism:

> Wir sitzen warm am Tische. In der Fibel
> Die Kinder blättern. Rings behaglich-stumm.
> Es trägt die Mutter auf den Suppenkübel.
> Der Vater bringt jetzt eine Henne um.
>
> Die Uhr, sie hinkt mit furchtbarem Gedröhn
> Durch Tag und Nacht. Da rauscht ein Sturm vorbei.
> Der Unterricht beginnt um Viertel zwei.
> Ein Telegramm verheisst den Sonntag schön.[7]
>
> We sit warm at the table. The children
> Are paging in their primers. All around cozy and quiet.
> The mother brings the soup pot in.
> The father is slaying a hen now.
>
> The clock, it limps with horrible rumbling
> Through day and night. A storm roars past.
> Classes begin at a quarter past one.
> A telegram promises a pleasant Sunday.

II *The New Morality/Anti-Wilhelminian Morality*

The Expressionist's special concern on this level focusses on the established attitude vis-à-vis sexuality. For him, as I pointed out in the discussion of Nietzsche's and Freud's influence in this area, this position is probably best characterized by the word "taboo." Wil-helminian society showed a basic fear of the power of the sexual drives when they were not locked up safely in the depths of man's psyche. It consequently made a concerted effort to suppress them, and to tacitly permit them to be satisfied in, at most, a clandestine (therefore, seemingly efficient and harmless) manner. In opposing this morality, the Expressionists were attempting to fulfill the prophecy of an earlier advocate of sexual freedom, Frank Wedekind, who had once written: "The next battle for freedom will be fought against the feudalism of love."

Wilhelminian society preferred to act as though its unofficial

apology for its "feudalistic" sexuality, the prostitute, did not exist.
And thus, the mere fact of the Expressionists' special, sympathetic
fondness for this figure in their literature was a direct affront to the
hypocrisy of convention. Poems on prostitutes, or poems in which
such figures play a significant role, were written by large numbers
of Expressionist poets, including Stramm, Werfel, Becher, Benn,
Ehrenstein, Blass, and Armin T. Wegner. Wegner's poem "Des
Dichters Lied von den Dirnen" ("The Poet's Song of the Strum-
pets," 1917), with its open declaration of the poet's kinship with
the prostitutes, probably exemplifies this theme best:

> Manchmal kommt eine Lust mich an,
> Den fremden Dirnen gleich in der Gasse
> Mich nächtens vor die Tore zu stellen.
> Möchte mich ihrer Schar gesellen,
> Flüsternd im Schatten der Häuserwand;
> Denn sie sind Schwestern und mir verwandt.[8]

> Sometimes a desire comes over me
> To stand at night before the entrance ways,
> Like the outcast strumpets in the streets.
> I'd like to join their hosts,
> Whispering in the shadows of the houses;
> For they are sisters and akin to me.

Explicit sensuality combined with a traditional religious theme in
Ball's "Der Henker" ("The Hangman") resulted in the Munich
authorities confiscating the issue of the biweekly *Revolution* in
which the poem appeared. The poem's opening lines, which de-
scribe some kind of wild, macabre orgy and then tie it into a highly
erotic treatment of the theme of the virgin birth, make it clear why
Germany's Catholic South found it so objectionable. Again, as
with the poems by Becher and Benn cited in the last section, Ball's
aim here is less to achieve profound poetic expression than to out-
rage and offend traditional moral and aesthetic taste; the poem's
blatant crudeness is thus intentional:

> Ich kugle Dich auf Deiner roten Decke.
> Ich bin am Werk: blank wie ein Metzgermeister.
> Tische und Bänke stehen wie blitzende Messer
> der Syphiliszwerg stochert in Töpfen voll Gallert
>   und Kleister.

Dein Leib ist gekrümmt und blendend und glänzt wie
    der gelbe Mond
deine Augen sind kleine lüsterne Monde
dein Mund ist geborsten in Wollust....[9]

I roll You on Your red blanket.
I'm at work: naked and shiny like a master butcher.
Tables and benches stand like sparkling knives — the syphilis
    dwarf pokes in pots of pulp and paste.
Your body is curved and dazzling and shines like the
    yellow moon
your eyes are small lustful moons
your mouth has burst in delight....

An equally intense strain of eroticism runs through most of the
verse in *Der Aufbruch* (1913), Stadler's only collection of poems
published during the Expressionist era. This collection of poems
seems to relate very systematically of the poet's development.
Central to his development is the awakening to sexuality and the
subsequent unrepressed experiencing of it (see, e.g., the poems
"Worte" — "Words," "Tage" — "Days," "Metamorphosen"
— "Metamorphoses," "Betörung" — "Delusion," "Was waren
Frauen," — "What were Women," "Fülle des Lebens," —
"Exuberance of Life"). But even more importantly, these exper-
iences are also the very ones that ultimately purify and sanctify his
life. The latter fact is given clearest expression in the poem
"Reinigung" ("Purification"):

Lausche: dein Blut will klingend in dir auferstehn! —
Fühlst du:
        schon schwemmt die starke Flut dich neu und rein,
Schon bist du selig in dir selbst allein
Und wie mit Auferstehungslicht umhangen —   .
Hörst du: schon ist die Erde um dich leer und weit
Und deine Seele atemlose Trunkenheit,
Die Morgenstimme deines Gottes zu umfangen.[10]

Listen: your blood is being resurrected joyfully in you! —
Do you feel:
        the strong tide is washing you fresh and pure now;
You are already at peace with yourself
And as though draped in the light of resurrection —
Do you hear: the earth is now empty and wide all around you

And your soul breathless intoxication,
Waiting to embrace the morning voice of your god.

Embracing the sensual life of man is also basic to Klemm's "summons" to follow him towards fulfillment in the collection of poems entitled *Aufforderung (Summons,* published in 1917 in Pfemfert's series "Die Aktions-Lyrik"). For Klemm, sensuality would seem to be the ruling principle in life. Thus, the "world traveler" in the poem "Weisheit" ("Wisdom") returns home with the look of fulfillment on his face: he has experienced all of life and "comprehended the meaning of earthly existence." And in the poem's closing lines we are evidently being allowed to share this knowledge as we see him embracing several alluring women:

> In seinem linken Arm schmiegen sich
> Nackt und reizend, zwei junge Weiber
> Zu denen er lächelnd sein Gesicht neigt
> Im rechten Arm schlummern ihm drei.[11]

> In his left arm are nestled
> Naked and enticing, two young women
> To whom he lowers his head with a smile;
> In his right arm three are slumbering.

I cited Becher's "Vorbereitung" in Chapter 4 as an illustration of the preoccupation of the Expressionist with visions of utopias as alternatives to Wilhelminian Germany. Becher's "Klänge aus Utopia" ("Sounds from Utopia," 1916) suggests that such a "New World" as that envisioned in "Vorbereitung" would be able to integrate love (in both the sensual and platonic sense) into life in a much more harmonious way than the old world had been able to. The image Becher presents of the men arriving in his utopia, welcomed by the women of the land, is couched in unmistakable fertility symbolism:

> O Mutterstadt im freien Morgenraum!
> Es flügeln Fenster an den Häuserfronten.
> Aus jedem Platz erwächst ein Brunnenbaum.
> Veranden segeln mondbeflaggte Gondeln.

> Sie künden Männer an, elastisch schwingen
> Die durch der Strassen ewig blaue Schlucht.

Ja —: Frauen schreitende! Mit Palmenfingern.
Geöffnet wie Kelche süssester Frucht.[12]

Oh native town in the open air of morning!
Windows swing out from the house fronts.
On every square a well stream shoots forth.
Verandas, moon-bedecked gondolas, set sail.

They herald the arrival of men; elastically
They swing through the narrow ever-blue streets.
Yes — Women striding! With palmlike fingers.
Opened wide like calyxes of sweetest fruit.

III   *The New Politics/Anti-Wilhelminian Politics*

From the outset, the Expressionists angrily rejected the society in which they had come of age. But they soon became aware that changing their society in a substantial way would require more than a change in its manners and morals. Several influential factors convinced them that they would have to radically alter its political and economic structures as well. These factors not only included the ideas of certain of their associates — members of the politically minded circle around Pfemfert's *Die Aktion* and political philosophers like Gustav Landauer *(Der Aufruf zum Sozialismus — The Call to Socialism,* 1911) and Kurt Eisner (premier of the short-lived Bavarian Soviet Republic of 1918-19) — but also certain central experiences — combat in the Great War, word of the events in Russia in 1917, involvement in their own revolution in November, 1918. Walter Hasenclever describes this ideological conversion from metaphysician to political idealist in a major poem of this phase, "Der politische Dichter" ("The Political Poet," 1917):

Der Dichter träumt nicht mehr in blauen Buchten.
Er sieht aus Höfen helle Schwärme reiten.
Sein Fuss bedeckt die Leichen der Verruchten.
Sein Haupt erhebt sich, Völker zu begleiten.[13]

The poet no longer dreams in fanciful seclusion.
He sees luminous throngs ride out of their courtyards.
His heel rests on the bodies of the infamous.
His head raised high, he prepares to escort the nations.

They needed concrete alternatives to the capitalist monarchy of

William II. Not unexpectedly they sought them at the opposite end of the political spectrum. They most frequently identified with the theories and principles of socialism, communism, anarchism, syndicalism, and pacifism.

Paul Zech was one of the earliest critics of the politico-economic base of Wilhelminian Germany in Expressionist poetry. His early political awakening was largely the outcome of work in European coal mines and active involvement in the union movement in coal-rich regions of Germany, Belgium, and northern France. These experiences took place mostly before the Expressionist era. His early verse, like that collected in *Das schwarze Revier (The Black District,* 1909, enlarged edition 1912) and *Die eiserne Brücke (The Iron Bridge,* 1914), depicts the inhuman and exploitative working conditions which he witnessed amongst the miners. "Fabrikstädte an der Wupper: Die andere Stadt" ("Factory Cities on the Wupper: The Other City") from the latter collection describes the sunless lives of the overtaxed and underpaid laborers in the "black cities" of Germany's industrial core, their plight even tacitly assented to by the churches and the small merchants:

> Schweiss kittet die bröckelnden Fugen fest;
> Schweiss aus vielerlei Blutsaft gegoren
> und ein Frommsein enteitert dem greisen Gebrest.
>
> Mancher hat hier sein Herz verludert, verloren;
> Kinder erzeugt mit schwachen Fraun...
> Doch die Kirchen und Krämer stehn hart wie aus Erz gehauen.[14]
>
> Sweat holds fast the crumbling frames;
> Sweat brewed of many men's blood
> And a pious life flows like pus from old sores.
>
> Many have wasted and lost their hearts here,
> Sired children with weak wives...
> Yet the churches and merchants stand solid as though
>   hewn from ore.

The large-scale appearance in later Expressionist literature of this kind of identification with the workers in Germany's great factories (identified as the proletariat, the misused, the downtrodden, and the outcast) provided the first clear signs of a general awakening to political and economic realities. We can follow this development, for example, in the verse of Becher, Otten, Goll, and Herrmann-Neisse.

For most Expressionists, this knowledge came most sharply and quickly once they had experienced the battlefields of World War I firsthand. War poems recording this lesson dominate Expressionist poetry in the period 1914-1918. The confrontation with inhumanity at the front marked a turning point in the development of such writers as Hasenclever, Oskar Kanehl, Rudolf Leonhard, Klemm, Ehrenstein, Lichtenstein, Stramm, and many others. Kanehl's verse from the war years, *Die Schande: Gedichte eines dienstpflichtigen Soldaten aus der Mordsaison 1914-18 (The Disgrace: Poems by a Draftee from the 1914-18 Era of Murder,* 1922) is a sharply accusatory document. He summarizes the lesson which the sight of bodies, mutilated and crippled by the war machine, taught him in the poem "An Alle" ("To All") from that collection:

> Soldaten! Alle!
> Entblösst Eure Narben auf den Marktplätzen.
> Reisst Eure Wunden auf.
> Hebt Eure Krücken, Kriegskrüppel, in den belebtesten Gassen.
> Kriegsblinde, Eure leeren Augenhöhlen.
> . . .
> Liebe zum Vaterland?
> . . .
> Bekennt:
> Der Mensch ist da.
> Der durch keinen Lohn und durch keine Drohungen zu
>   bewegen ist
> Gegen den Mitmenschen zu sein.
> Der Mensch ist da.
> Der den Mitmenschen liebt wie sich selbst.
> Der den Mitmenschen dient, wie sich selbst.
> Dessen Berufung die Arbeit ist
> Zur Erhöhung des Menschen.
> Bekennt:
> Wir sind vaterlandslos.... [15]

> Soldiers! All!
> Expose your scars on the market places.
> Tear open your wounds.
> Raise your crutches, victims of war, in the most
>   crowded streets.
> Those blinded in war, your empty eye sockets.

. . .
Love for the fatherland?

. . .
Acknowledge:
Man has come.
Who is to be moved by no wages and threats
To be against his fellow man.
Man has come.
Who loves his fellow man as himself
Who serves his fellow man as himself.
Whose mission is to work
For the elevation of man.
Acknowledge:
We have no fatherland. . . .

The last poem in that volume, "Revolution," offers Kanehl's solution to the political and economic conditions that had produced the war; a form of social-democratic rule by the masses:

Gerottet wie Gewitterwolken
Volk.
Umdrohen sie den morschen Staat.
Und zucken auf und schlagen ein.
Volk.

Der Thron ist leer. Der Altar leer.
Volk.
Lasst Knechte uns regieren.
Und Huren Mütter Gottes sein.
Volk.

Blut trieft von unsern Knochenhänden.
Volk.
Auf Königsleichen stehn wir stolz.
Rot deckt die ganze Erde unsre Fahne.
Volk.[16]

Assembled like storm clouds
People.
They threaten the rotten state.
And flare up and strike out.
People.

The throne is empty. The altar empty.
People.

Let slaves govern us.
And whores be the mothers of God.
People.

Blood drips from our bony hands.
People.
We stand proud on carcasses of kings.
Our flag covers the earth red.
People.

Kanehl's answer is also typical of most Expressionist political verse in this phase: that his revolution is guided by, and directed toward the realization of, socialist or communist principles is alluded to only in the color of the flag which the revolutionaries are carrying. Similarly, Becher's only clear reference to a tangible political goal in the revolution called for in "Ewig im Aufruhr," comes in the same kind of image at the close of his poem: "Fahnen hissen sich/Heilig in Rot" ("Flags are raised/Sacred in red").

Other Expressionist poets are only slightly more literal, combining such chromatic allusions to the ideal state with direct references to a "republic." Thus, the flag of the revolution led by Hasenclever's ideal poet in "Der politische Dichter" is also red. We realize that the final political goal of the revolution is to be a socialist republic when we are told in a later stanza:

Er wird ihr Führer sein. Er wird verkünden.
Die Flamme seines Wortes wird Musik.
Er wird den grossen Bund der Staaten gründen.
Das Recht des Menschentums. Republik.[17]

He will be their leader. He will proclaim.
The flame of his words will be music.
He will found the great union of states.
The rights of mankind. The Republic.

The goal of Leonhard's revolution as outlined in his poem "Vereinigung der Räterepubliken" ("Union of the Soviet Republics," 1921) is identified in a similar manner:

. . .   Die ganze Erde
ein Bund liebender Räterepubliken,
wo ewig Wandern aller Wurzeln bliebe,

und jeder blüht, und jegliche Beschwerde
in aller Brüder Armen muss ersticken:
das Rot des Blutes gibt das Tuch der Liebe.[18]

. . .   The whole earth
a union of benevolent soviet republics,
where the passage of our roots would stay forever,

and everyone flourishes, and all complaints
are stifled in the arms of all brothers:
the red of blood yields the fabric of love.

By its very nature as the most subjective medium of literary expression, the lyric poem does not lend itself effectively to concrete or detailed political statement. Expressionist political poetry is, therefore, often highly abstract or even cryptic. But such a medium was only one of the ways these poets found to give expression to a newly found political consciousness: all but a very few of them also threw their active support behind the left-wing leadership of the revolution which toppled the Wilhelminian monarchy in 1918.

IV   *The New Vision/Anti-Wilhelminian World View*

Pinthus and other theorists of the movement describe the Expressionist interpretation of the established world view of Wilhelminian Germany: it was a view based on an "imaginary" or arbitrary reality which had been created by a special set of political, economic, and technological circumstances. It was, moreover, ultimately conditioned by principles derived from the modern natural, physical, and mathematical sciences. Its basis was positivist, materialist, and determinist. All things were considered predetermined or governed by a set of concrete and ultimately measurable (empirical) factors. All other "realities" which could not be accomodated or measured by it on its own terms were "destroyed," as Benn put it in a later, nostalgic memoir on Expressionism ("Bekenntnis zum Expressionismus" — "Commitment to Expressionism," 1933). For the Expressionist, such a perspective on the world was narrow, limiting, and shallow. It was especially insensitive to such intangibles as spiritual and metaphysical idealities ("das Herz" — "the heart," "die Seele" — "the soul," "der Geist" — "the spirit"), nonlogical thought processes (paradox, contradiction), the life of the instincts. Expressionist literature responded by trying to penetrate through its "imaginary" surface and to point to other realities beyond.

The most subtle of these responses was the use of disrupted perspective or unconventional imagery. In such poetry, the Expressionist poet in general only alludes to his alternative vision by undermining the security of the conventional world view through his unsettling sensitivity to the power of intangible forces. Hoddis's "Weltende," Heym's "Der Gott der Stadt" and "Ophelia" and Lichtenstein's "Die Dämmerung," cited in the previous chapter, are some of the most noteworthy poems of this type. The importance of their example for the development of Expressionist verse can be illustrated by Becher's "Gesang vor Morgen" ("Song before Morning," 1914). The title of the poem is, of course, vaguely reminiscent of Heym's and Hoddis's. The only significant difference between Becher's poem and its models is perhaps the fact that his premonitions of doom are considerably more gruesome:

> Da kotzt auf Dächer Mondes schiefer Mund
> Gallgrünen Schleim. Noch Autobusse zögern.
> Die Strasse heult, ein aufgeteilter Hund,
> Dadurch wir waten dünn mit Aktenschmökern.
>
> In hohen Lüften Kohlenhaufen glosen.
> Der Wolken graue Röcke weisen Schlitze.
> Geschwollene Scham quillt auf ein Himmel rosen,
> In dessen Fleisch wohl krumme Messer blitzen.
>
> Die Mörder unter düsterem Baldachin
> An Galgen baumeln, schlagend oft zusammen.
> Auf Plätze klatschen Kübel Blutes hin.
> Der Häuser Hüften peitschen Scharlachflammen.
>
> Die Huren sammeln sich vor blinder Kneipe,
> Wie Vogelscheuchen flatternd auf dem Felde,
> Die klappern in der Morgenwinde Kälte. —
> Wir werden uns an fernem Ort entleiben.[19]

> The wry mouth of the moon pukes on roofs
> Gall-green slime. Buses pause.
> The street howls, a dismembered dog;
> We wade through it thinly with worthless papers.

In the high air coal piles smolder.
The clouds' gray skirts reveal slits.
Swollen genitals swell pink across the sky,
In whose flesh crooked knives flash.

The murderers under gloomy baldachin
Dangle on gallows, knocking together often.
Buckets of blood splash onto squares.
Scarlet flames lash the hips of houses.

The whores gather before a misty bar,
Like scarecrows fluttering on a field,
That flap in the cold of morning winds. —
We shall slay ourselves at some distant place.

In his poetry, Klemm decried the neglect of man's spiritual
needs. And in "Meine Zeit" ("My Age," 1917), he argues that it is
a fateful neglect, for it accounts for the tragically rent state of con-
temporary life, modern man's loss of faith and his profound ignor-
ance about the nature of existence:

In Wolkenfernen trommeln die Propeller.
Völker zerfliessen. Bücher werden Hexen.
Die Seele schrumpft zu winzigen Komplexen.
Tot ist die Kunst. Die Stunden kreisen schneller.

O meine Zeit! So namenlos zerrissen,
So ohne Stern, so daseinsarm im Wissen
wie du, will keine, keine mir erscheinen.[20]

The propellers rumble in the distant clouds.
Nations dissolve. Books become witches.
The soul shrinks to minute complexes.
Art is dead. The hours spin faster.

Oh, my age. So utterly divided,
So without star, so poor in vital knowledge
As you, none other, none other seems to be.

This neglect of the spirit, Klemm believes, stems from modern
man's obsession with the kind of technological advances to which
he alludes in the lines just quoted. In his poem "Erscheinung"
("Appearance," 1917), Klemm locates the root of this narrow interest
in the notion that all questions and needs of man can be an-

swered or met by material reality. But the "shadows" from the past who attend the banquet in this poem, enveloping "whole worlds" in the folds of their garments, give the lie to the Wilhelminian world view by the simple fact of their being:

> Tor, wer glaubt zwischen Sohle und Scheitel
> Sei alles beschlossen, was Mensch genannt wird!
> Des Herzens unauslöschlicher Drang, die Geisterarme,
> Die hinausgreifen nach den Ringen an den Pforten Gottes!
> Du mit dem Fabelblick, — atmest du Ewigkeit?
> Und du schönes Profil voll Schwermut, neigst du die Stirn
> Tiefer lauschend in die Schneckenwindungen des Himmels?[21]

> Fool, who thinks between heel and crown
> All things are resolved that are called man!
> The inextinguishable will of the heart, the arms of spirits
> That reach out for the rings on the gates of God!
> You with the dreamer's look — Do you breathe eternity?
> And you, beautiful face full of melancholy, do you lower
>   your head,
> Listening more intently to the spirallings of heaven?

Much like Werfel, Wolfenstein, Hasenclever, Goll, Lasker-Schüler, Kurt Heynicke, and many other Expressionist poets, Otten emphasizes the need for restoring to this world the values associated with the "heart" (love, sympathy, warmth, friendship, sensitivity, etc.). In his "Thronerhebung des Herzens" (Enthronement of the Heart," 1917) he admonishes his fellow man:

> Schlage dein Herz auf, Bruder:
> Das Buch der Morgenröte, Bruder
> Der neuen Zeit, Bruder
> Den Mantel der Furcht, Bruder
> Das Auge der Erkenntnis, Bruder![22]

> Open your heart up, brother:
> The book of the dawn, brother
> Of the new age, brother
> The cloak of fear, brother
> The eye of knowledge, brother!

The revolt that Heynicke calls for in his "Aufbruch" ("Breaking Away," 1918) is one that manifests itself simply in a "breaking out" of the darkness into the light through the exercise of the illuminating powers of love:

> Es blüht die Welt.
> Ja, hocherhoben, Herz, wach auf!
> Erhellt die Welt,
> zerschellt die Nacht,
> brich auf ins Licht!
>
> In die Liebe, Herz, brich auf.
> Mit guten Augen leuchte Mensch zu Mensch.
> . . .[23]
>
> The world is in bloom
> Yes, raised on high, awaken, heart!
> Illume the world;
> smash the night;
> break out into the light!
>
> Into love, break out, heart.
> Radiate with benevolent eyes from man to man.
> . . .

In many of her poems, Lasker-Schüler lamented that the Wilhelminian positivist reality was for her unbearably dismal and restricting, threatening to stifle and destroy her. She announced her longing to withdraw from it in a very early poem, "Weltflucht" ("Flight from the World," 1902):

> Ich will in das Grenzenlose
>   Zu mir zurück,
> Schon blüht die Herbstzeitlose
>   Meiner Seele,
> Vielleicht — ist's schon zu spät zurück!
> O, ich sterbe unter Euch!
> Da Ihr mich erstickt mit Euch.
> . . .[24]
>
> I want to return to the boundlessness
>   that is in me;
> The autumn flower of timelessness* is blossoming now
>   in my soul;

---

*die Herbstzeitlose = (literally) 'meadow-saffron' or 'autumn crocus,' but the word's parts suggest more importantly the allusions I record.

Perhaps — it is too late to go back!
Oh, I am dying amidst You!
Since You're stifling me with You.

. . .

But, like Otten and Heynicke, she eventually found a sometimes consoling alternative by fusing a unique kind of religious mysticism with the values of the "heart." In a much later poem, "Gebet" ("Prayer," 1917), she declares:

Ich habe Liebe in die Welt gebracht —
Dass blau zu blühen jedes Herz vermag,
Und hab ein Leben müde mich gewacht,
In Gott gehüllt den dunklen Atemschlag.[25]

I have brought love into the world —
So that each heart can spread blue blossoms,
And have sat watch till tired my whole life long,
My dark breath enveloped in God.

Benn was probably most caustic and constant in criticism of the established Wilhelminian order. Much of his early verse especially concentrates on efforts to penetrate and expose the established world view. In "Das Plakat" ("The Placard," 1917) he attacks Western civilization's self-deceptive reliance on conventional logic (line 3), mathematics (line 5), medicine (line 6), modern industry (line 7), and political structures (line 9) to solve all of its problems:

Früh, wenn der Abendmensch ist eingepflügt
und bröckelt mit der kalten Stadt im Monde;
wenn Logik nicht im ethischen Konnex,
nein, kategorisch wuchtet; Mangel an Aufschwung
Bejahung stänkert, Klammerung an Zahlen
(zumal wenn teilbar), Einbeinung in den Gang
nach Krankenhaus, Fabrik, Registratur
im Knie zu Hausbesitzverein, Geschlechtsbejahung,
Fortpflanzung, staatlichem Gemeinsystem
ingrimmige Bekennung —
tröstet den Trambahngast
allein das farbenprächtige Plakat.[26]

Early, when Western man is plowed in
and crumbles with the cold city in the moon;
when logic weighs heavy, not in the
ethical code, but categorically; lack of enthusiasm
affirmation causing a stink, clinging to numbers
(especially if divisible), locked into the walk
to hospital, factory, registry
on his knees to landlord's union, affirming sex,
procreation, state welfare system
wrathful avowal —
the tram rider is consoled
only by the colorful placard.

In his poetry, Benn generally defined the one-sidedness of the conventional vision as an excessive and even arrogant deference to man's cerebral faculties. In "Synthese" ("Synthesis," 1917) he caricatures the self-assured, intellect-oriented man (lines 1-4), who looks condescendingly back on his animal beginnings (lines 5-6) and experiences all things (even sexuality) in narcissistic delight (lines 7-8):

Schweigende Nacht. Schweigendes Haus.
Ich aber bin der stillsten Sterne,
ich treibe auch mein eignes Licht
noch in die eigne Nacht hinaus.

Ich bin gehirnlich heimgekehrt
aus Höhlen, Himmeln, Dreck und Vieh.
Auch was sich noch der Frau gewährt,
ist dunkle süsse Onanie.[27]

Reticent night. Reticent house.
But I am of the stillest stars,
and I thrust out my self-made light
out into my self-made night.

I have returned home in brain
from caves, heavens, filth and beast.
Even what is still bestowed on woman
is dark and sweet onanism.

Benn's alternative is a return to a total submersion of the self in the life of the instincts and the dissolution of the "ego" ("das Ich," "der Ich-Begriff"), the divisive, conscious self. In his poetry,

he generally associates the life of the instincts with certain meta-
phoric code words, such as "das Blut" ("the blood"), "das Meer"
("the sea"), and "die Olive" ("the olive tree"). Often his imagery
will situate it geographically in tropical or southern climes, as in the
opening stanza of "Reise" ("Journey," 1916):

> O dieses Lichts! Die Insel kränzt
> sternblaues Wasser um sich her,
> am Saum gestillt, zu Strand ergänzt,
> und sättigt täglich sich am Meer.[28]

> Oh, this light! Star-blue water
> forms a wreath around the island,
> breaking softly where the shore begins,
> which daily drinks its fill of the sea.

V   *The New Man/Anti-Wilhelminian Man*

How the Expressionists envision the overcoming of the Wil-
helminian image of man and the realization of the new man already
inheres in what I have said about their assessment of the contem-
porary world. In fact, the Expressionist image of the new man was
most often only implicit in criticism of the "old man." This new
man is generally the individual who has the knowledge and critical
vision to recognize and expose the evils and weaknesses of his
world. He possesses the "illumination" ("Erhelltsein") which, for
example, qualifies him for a position of leadership in the revolution
that Lotz describes in "Aufbruch der Jugend." For Werfel, the
new man is most importantly one who is particularly sensitive to
the basic human qualities in himself and his fellow man (see "Ein
Lebenslied" — "A Song of Life," 1913), who possesses a great
love for mankind (see "An den Leser," cited in the Prologue) and
who will exult in the knowledge that he has done a good deed for
another man's benefit (see "Ich habe eine gute Tat getan" — "I
have done a good deed," 1911).[29] But he is additionally a man who
has a unique knowledge, an "illumed vision," of the contemporary
world's flaws and of life's higher significance. Werfel describes him
in these terms in the poem "Der schöne strahlende Mensch" ("The
Beautiful Radiant Man," 1911):

> Ich bin ein Korso auf besonnten Plätzen,
> Ein Sommerfest mit Frauen und Bazaren,
> Mein Auge bricht von allzuviel Erhelltsein.[30]

> I am a corso on sunlit squares;
> A summer fair with women and bazaars;
> My eye is blinded by an excess of illumination.

Because Werfel's new man possesses all of the special qualities we have just outlined, he not only enjoys great harmony and happiness himself but is also able to imbue the world with such qualities. That same poem begins:

> Die Freunde, die mit mir sich unterhalten,
> Sonst oft missmutig, leuchten vor Vergnügen,
> Lustwandeln sie in meinen schönen Zügen
> Wohl Arm in Arm, veredelte Gestalten.

> Ach, mein Gesicht kann niemals Würde halten,
> Und Ernst und Gleichmut will ihm nicht genügen,
> Weil tausend Lächeln in erneuten Flügen
> Sich ewig seinem Himmelsbild entfalten.

> The friends, who converse with me,
> Cast off their bad spirits and radiate with delight,
> When they enjoy a stroll in the beauty of my features,
> Perhaps arm in arm, ennobled figures.

> Oh, my face can never maintain dignity,
> And gravity and composure cannot suffice it,
> Since a thousand smiles in renewed flights
> Eternally unfold from its firmament.

For the Expressionist, the ultimate goal of the new man is to embody the ideals Werfel describes and to provide for their dissemination. The achievement of this goal involves transcending the limits of conventional Wilhelminian life and embracing a broader spectrum of experience than represented by convention. As I have already suggested, for Benn this means breaking the hold which man's cerebral perspective has on experience, and totally embracing man's primeval, preconscious existence. This philosophy lies at the root of his plea for the "Urwaldmensch," who delights in the enjoyment of his basic appetites, in the poem "Alaska" cited earlier. In a poem which dates from the same year, "Gesänge" ("Songs," 1913), Benn puts it in terms of an atavistic longing to return to man's origins in the sea:

O dass wir unsere Ururahnen wären.
Ein Klümpchen Schleim in einem warmen Moor.
Leben und Tod, Befruchten und Gebären
glitte aus unseren stummen Säften vor.[31]

Oh, if only we were our primeval ancestors.
A little clump of slime in a warm moor.
Life and death, fertilization and birth
would glide forth from our mute secretions.

Goll's atavism in *Der neue Orpheus (The New Orpheus,* 1918) is much more conservative than Benn's. In this seven-part dithyramb,[32] written in the long, loosely structured lines of Walt Whitman, he suggests that the restoration of harmony in existence need not require a reversion to man's primordial origins in the sea, merely that all men honestly embrace once more their common earthly essence. In the prophetic vision of the poem, the music of Orpheus, who is profoundly sensitive to all qualities of life and all levels of experience, revives in man the ability again to hear "the breath of the earth," "the eternal murmurings in men." At the poem's close, mankind, now reunited, is led by Goll's twentieth-century charmer out of his dark and lonely existence in the "underworld" of the modern, industrial cities up into the saving grace of light and therewith into eternity:

Der Himmel war niedergekommen. Die Menschen küssten sich.

Fern in Nacht und Geschichte lag die tägliche Unterwelt.
Orpheus der Befreier sang. Er führte die Menschheit hinaus zur Absolution.[33]

Heaven had descended. The people kissed each other.

Far away in night and history lay the everyday underworld.
Orpheus the liberator sang. He led mankind out to absolution.

Trakl's position is similar. He reveres the simple life, the life of the farmer, the hunter, and the shepherd, a life uncluttered and unsullied by modern civilization. His poem "Kaspar Hauser Lied" ("Song of Kaspar Hauser," 1913) is a poignant juxtaposition of these two opposing worlds. Trakl uses the figure of the wild boy who appeared mysteriously one day in 1828 in a German city as an image of primeval man. The original, ideal state of existence seems suggested in the purity (line 5) and righteousness (line 15), in the nearness to nature (lines 1-4, 14, 17) and to God (lines 6-7) which Kaspar enjoyed before he was destroyed by an insensitive Western civilization (lines 8, 12-13):

> Er wahrlich liebte die Sonne, die purpurn den Hügel
>   hinabstieg,
> Die Wege des Walds, den singenden Schwarzvogel
> Und die Freude des Grüns.
>
> Ernsthaft war sein Wohnen im Schatten des Baums
> Und rein sein Antlitz.
> Gott sprach eine sanfte Flamme zu seinem Herzen:
> O Mensch!
>
> Stille fand sein Schritt die Stadt am Abend;
> Die dunkle Klage seines Munds:
> Ich will ein Reiter werden.
>
> Ihm aber folgte Busch und Tier,
> Haus und Dämmergarten weisser Menschen
> Und sein Mörder suchte nach ihm.
>
> Frühling und Sommer und schön der Herbst
> Des Gerechten, sein leiser Schritt
> An den dunklen Zimmern Träumender hin.
> Nachts blieb er mit seinem Stern allein;
>
> Sah, dass Schnee fiel in kahles Gezweig
> Und im dämmernden Hausflur den Schatten des Mörders.
>
> Silbern sank des Ungebornen Haupt hin.[34]
>
> He truly loved the sun, which descended the hill in a
>   purple glow,
> The paths of the forest, the singing blackbird
> And the joys of the verdure.
>
> His sojourn in the shade of the tree was grave
> And his countenance pure.
> God spake a soft flame to his heart:
> Ah! Man!
>
> His footstep found the city still in the evening;
> The dark lament of his voice:
> I want to be a rider.

But bush and animal followed him,
House and dusky garden of white men
And his murderer sought him.

Spring and summer and beautiful the autumn
Of the righteous, his soft footstep
Past the dark rooms of dreamers.
At night he was alone with his star;

Saw that snow fell on barren branches
And the shadow of the murderer in dusky hallway.

Silverly the head of the unborn sank back.

A related group of poets, including most prominently Lasker-Schüler, Stramm, Nebel, Franz Behrens, Heynicke, and other members of the circle around Walden's *Der Sturm,* states the means to achieving the essence of the new man in the form of a fusion of the self with the cosmos, with the totality of the universe. Lasker-Schüler expressed a desire for such a feeling of oneness with all things in the poem "Versöhnung" ("Reconciliation," 1911). As in much of her poetry, this feeling is inseparable from her sense of being one with God through the expression of love:

> Es wird ein grosser Stern in meinen Schoss fallen...
> Wir wollen wachen die Nacht,
>   . . .
> Wir wollen uns versöhnen die Nacht —
> So viel Gott strömt über.
>   . . .
> Wir wollen uns versöhnen die Nacht,
> Wenn wir uns herzen, sterben wir nicht.[35]

> A great star will fall into my lap...
> We shall keep watch this night,
>   . . .
> We shall have a reconciliation this night —
> Since so much of God is overflowing.
>   . . .
> We shall have a reconciliation this night;
> If we embrace each other, we will not die.

August Stramm records the realization of such a desire — also by means of a similar sense of harmony in profound love relationships (suggested here by the "Du") — in the terse language of "Wunder" ("Miracle," 1914):

> Du steht! Du steht!
> Und ich
> Und ich
> Ich winge
> Raumlos zeitlos wäglos
> Du steht! Du steht!
> Und Rasen bäret mich
> Ich
> Bär mich selber!
> Du!
> Du!
> Du bannt die Zeit
> Du bogt der Kreis
> Du seelt der Geist
> Du blickt der Blick
> Du
> Kreist die Welt
> Die Welt
> Die Welt!
> Ich
> Kreis das All!
> Und du
> Und du
> Du stehst
> Das
> Wunder![36]

> Thou stands! Thou stands!
> And I
> And I
> I wing
> Spaceless timeless weighless
> Thou stands! Thou stands!
> And raging bears me
> I
> Bear my very self!
> Thou!
> Thou!
> Thou transfixes time
> Thou arches the ring
> Thou ensouls the spirit

Thou casts the glance
Thou
Rings the world
The world
The world!
I
Ring the all!
And thou
And thou
Thou standst
The
Miracle!

The close thematic, as well as stylistic, uniformity of the work of members of the *Sturm* circle is made clear by a comparison of Heynicke's poem "Mensch" ("Man," written before 1920) with Stramm's in this context. Heynicke's ideal is man conceived of as an extension of the totality of the universe which, at the highest level, is the equivalent of God ("dem hohen All-Kreisenden," "Er"):

Ich bin über den Wäldern,
grün und leuchtend,
hoch über allen,
ich, der Mensch.
Ich bin Kreis im All,
. . .
ich fühle mich tief,
nahe dem hohen All-Kreisenden,
ich, sein Gedanke.
. . .
ich leuchte,
ich,
wie Er,
das All;
das All,
wie ich![37]

I am above the forests,
green and radiant,
high above everyone,
I, man.
I am a ring in the all,

. . .
I feel deeply,
near the all-orbiter,
I, his thought.
. . .
I radiate,
I,
as He,
the all;
the all,
as I!

Finally, we should mention one other major group of Expressionist poets who conceived of the realization of the new man's goal in the form of a blending of all of the basic qualities of human character and experience: the intellectual and emotional, civilized and primitive, spiritual and material. Becher describes the creation of such a "new man" in "Aufruf zum Neuen Mensch" ("Call for the New Man," 1919). Here, the opposing spheres of character and experience that are to be fused so as to produce a higher form of man are alluded to in two parallel stanzas: in the first, they are depicted as intellectual or spiritual striving versus the physical sensations; in the second, as the "northern" versus the "southern" and the "middle" races:

Euer Kristallhaupt gesetzt zum Turm den unendlichen
    Breiten!
Bambus-Haine schlagen raschelnd Gongs an die Gewölke
    euerer Rippen —
Himalaja-Turban. Niagara: Schleifen kühlen euch brennende
    Gelenke...

Baut euch auf! Menschen! Menschen aus Fels! Menschen
    bitteren Pols!
Bumerang-Menschen; o Lasso-Menschen, o Menschen nörd-
    licheren, südlicheren, mittleren Grads!
Menschen aller Breiten, vereinigt euch:
Ein Mensch ersteht: welch ein Typ! Aller Kreaturen
    Geliebter und Erzfreund....[38]

Your crystal heads are towers overlooking the bound-
    less expanses!
Bamboo groves, rustling gongs beat against the mass of your ribs —
Himalaya turban. Niagara: bows cool your burning joints....

Build yourselves up! Mankind! Cliff dwellers! People of the icy pole!
Boomerang people; oh, lasso people, oh, people of the more
    northern, southern, middle latitudes!
People of all the hemispheres, unite!
A man is born — What a specimen! Cherished and befriended by
all. . . .

The "idealist" who addresses the reader in Klemm's poem "Der
Idealist" (1917) assumes a position closely related to Becher's. He
embraces wholeheartedly and (as the title of the poem would seem
to want to indicate) optimistically the two opposing, contradictory
"directions" of man's striving, one upward (spiritual or intellec-
tual) and the other downward (material or sensual):

> . . .
> Das ist die Tragik meines Daseins. Aber vielleicht
>   grade deshalb
> Bin ich so wahnsinnig grossartig in den beiden
>   Richtungen,
>
> In die mir zu wachsen vergönnt ist, und so treibe ich
> Todesmutig empor meinen rasenden Strahl,
> Mit furchtbarer Kraft Löcher stossend ins Firmament:
> Raum, jetzt komme ich!
>
> Meinen Schaft stürz' ich hinab, saugenden Rüssel,
> Dass die Tiefe der Hölle aufschluchzt in seinen Schacht,
> Säule bin ich, Phallus, Hals ohne Haupt und Rumpf:
> Welch himmlische Sense will mich mähen?[39]

> . . .
> That is the tragedy of my existence. But perhaps that
>   is exactly why
> I am so insanely masterful in both directions,
>
> In which I am allowed to grow, and thus defying death
> I drive my mad beam of light upwards,
> Penetrating the firmament with tremendous force —
> Space, now I am coming!
>
> I cast my shaft downwards, a trunk which
> Sucks up into it the abyss of hell;
> I am a column, phallus, neck without head or torso —
> What heavenly scythe shall reap me?

The five thematic complexes just outlined are naturally only as neatly differentiated as they were above in the critic's perception; individual literary works are generally less transparent and always more encompassing than I may seem to have suggested. The last thematic group referred to will probably have demonstrated by itself that all the themes are intimately interwoven and interrelated. We can establish several things they have in common if we consider them from a broader perspective.

All Expressionists were trying in their own particular way to break out of established society through a critical penetration of its boundaries. Thus, implicitly when not explicitly, they all rejected the consensus view of reality, morality, politics, the world, and man because they found it too narrow and self-interested. Their goal was to overcome its frustrating restrictions and to bridge the gap between its painful divisions. They were reaching for a more inclusive, reconciling view of life and a wider scale of experience. They wanted to expand the scope of their lives and attain a fuller appreciation of existence than they felt was being permitted them by convention in Wilhelminian Germany. If we are looking, then, for a term that will circumscribe the general thematic axis of Expressionism, the most adequate is no doubt the one offered by some of the Expressionists themselves: "totality."[40]

CHAPTER 7

Conclusion

THE approach to poetry in this study was broad; it was often
necessary to sacrifice detail for the sake of scope, and depth for
the sake of breadth. This was unavoidable, because the purpose
was to survey not only Expressionist poetry, but also the whole
movement which it represented. The basic principle that guided this
investigation was the thesis that one body of literature cannot be
distinguished from another on purely literary grounds. Styles and
themes in literature are not bound to history; rather, they are vir-
tually universal. Thus, stylistic techniques such as perceptual dis-
tortion, startling imagery, condensation of language, and thematic
tendencies such as a concern with the divisions in life, the desire to
revise external reality, visions of impending doom, are found in
other phases of German literary history. To determine the unique-
ness of a body of literature, we have to exceed the limits of specifi-
cally literary criteria and also consider literature's relationship to its
general historical background. We have to do this, furthermore, if
we wish to properly appreciate a literature per se. For, like litera-
ture itself, literary study cannot be executed in a historical vacuum.

This approach has made it possible to establish that the Expres-
sionists were responding in their poetry to their historical situation.
In this special combination of conditioning factors, they all came
of age and found the basic impulse for their attitudes and actions.
Together they argued certain issues which their society had raised
and rejected, or advocated certain resolutions that their society ren-
dered potentially relevant. They made their own direct contribution
to history by communicating their positions on their times in many
ways, but most especially through art, using literary means culled
from both the present and the past. Most of these activities were
characterized by a high degree of congruency and concertedness
among the artists involved. Expressionists and critics alike have

therefore correctly described these activities with the term "literary movement."

This conception of historical uniqueness and literary cohesiveness is naturally more involved than a mere list of stylistic and thematic features. But it does more justice, I think, to the literature as a product of human endeavor. Moreover, by reestablishing the historical meaningfulness of the literature, I think it also does best justice to the individual poets and poems of Expressionism.

In the last few decades, Expressionist literature has seldom been dealt with critically as anything but the raw material for the self-serving analyses of literary scholarship. However, if we read this literature as a product of a total human condition, thereby rejustifying its existence, this will help it to speak to us again as vital literary statement. In other words, we will perhaps be able to identify with it as human artistic expression, which offers us a perspective on an era unlike that offered by any other medium, and which we can judge as being now more, now less valid for our own time. In that way we can learn and profit more from it as history. A collection of mini-interpretations of individual poems could not have achieved that result. I hope, on the other hand, that the reader will be able to execute such interpretations more easily by himself after having read this study.

Notes and References

Chronology

This chronology is indebted in part to the following publications: *Expressionismus: Aufzeichnungen und Erinnerungen der Zeitgenossen,* ed. Paul Raabe (Olten and Freiburg im Breisgau, 1965); *Expressionismus: Literatur und Kunst: 1910-1923: Eine Ausstellung des deutschen Literaturarchivs im Schiller-Nationalmuseum Marbach a.N.,* Catalogue No. 7, Sonderausstellungen des Schiller-Nationalmuseums, ed. Bernhard Zeller, et al. (Marbach a.N., 1960); Roy F. Allen, *Literary Life in German Expressionism and the Berlin Circles* (Göppingen, 1974).

Chapter One

1. A major exception to the failure of handbooks to help us in understanding the concept is Harry Shaw, *Dictionary of Literary Terms* (New York, 1972), pp. 246-47. See also Allen, *Literary Life,* pp. 18-19.

2. *The Random House Dictionary of the English Language* (New York, 1969), pp. 936-37.

3. Allen, *Literary Life,* pp. 20-24, *passim.*

4. Theodor Däubler, *Im Kampf um die moderne Kunst* (Berlin, 1919), p. 42.

5. Armin Arnold, *Die Literatur des Expressionismus: Sprachliche und thematische Quellen* (Stuttgart, 1966), p. 11.

6. Walter Serner, "Die neue Sezession," *Die Aktion,* II (1912), columns 173-76.

7. Cited in *Expressionismus: Der Kampf um eine literarische Bewegung,* ed. Paul Raabe (Munich, 1965), p. 296.

8. *Ibid.,* pp. 41, 43; Paul Pörtner, *Literatur-Revolution 1910-1925,* II (Neuwied a.R. and Berlin-Spandau, 1961), pp. 171, 177, 178; Ernst Stadler, *Dichtungen,* ed. Karl Ludwig Schneider (Hamburg, n.d. [1954]), II, p. 35; Hugo Ball, *Flight Out of Time: A Dada Diary,* ed. John Elderfield and trans. Ann Raimes (New York, 1974), p. 9.

9. See *Expressionismus: Der Kampf,* ed. Raabe, pp. 52-146; Pörtner, pp. 181ff.

10. The substantial collections of these writings in the volumes cited in the footnote above are only a small sampling. Virtually every issue of each of the Expressionist journals included a theoretical essay. These writings

are indexed in *Index Expressionismus: Bibliographie der Beiträge in den Zeitschriften und Jahrbüchern des literarischen Expressionismus, 1910-1925,* ed. Paul Raabe, Vols. I-XVIII (Nendeln-Liechtenstein, 1972).

Chapter Two

1. Hugo von Hofmannsthal, "Poesie und Leben," rpt. in *Ars Poetica,* ed. Beda Allemann (Darmstadt, 1966), p. 13.
2. Kurt Pinthus, "Zur jüngsten Dichtung," rpt. in *Expressionismus: Der Kampf,* ed. Raabe, p. 78.
3. Pinthus stated this position for Expressionism more directly in 1919: "Never was the aesthetic and the principle of 'l'art pour l'art' so disdained as in this poetry, which we call the 'most recent' or 'Expressionist,' because it is completely eruption, explosion, intensity — it must be that way in order to shatter the inimical crust [of realtiy]." See *Menschheitsdämmerung: Ein Dokument des Expressionismus,* ed. Kurt Pinthus (Hamburg, 1972), p. 29.
4. Stefan George, *Das Jahr der Seele* (Düsseldorf, 1964), p. 12.
5. *Menschheitsdämmerung,* ed. Pinthus, p. 279.
6. On Whitman's influence on Expressionist poetry, see below, Chapter 5 and Reinhold Grimm and Henry J. Schmidt, "Foreign Influences on German Expressionist Poetry," in *Expressionism as an International Literary Phenomenon,* ed. Ulrich Weisstein (Paris and Budapest, 1973), pp. 69-78.
7. Wassily Kandinsky, *Concerning the Spiritual in Art,* trans. M.T.H. Sadler (New York, 1977), p. 1.
8. Kasimir Edschmid, "Über die dichterische deutsche Jugend," in Kasimir Edschmid, *Über den Expressionismus in der Literatur und die neue Dichtung,* Die Tribüne der Kunst and Zeit, no. 1 (Berlin, 1920), p. 24.

Chapter Three

1. Peter N. Stearns, *European Society in Upheaval: Social History Since 1800* (New York, 1967), pp. 55-359.
2. The major sources for remarks on the general social, political, and economic background of the period are: Karl Erich Born, "Der soziale und wirtschaftliche Strukturwandel Deutschlands am Ende des 19. Jarhhunderts," in *Moderne deutsche Socialgeschichte,* ed. Hans-Ulrich Wehler (Cologne, 1966), pp. 271-284; *Das Wilhelminische Deutschland: Stimmen der Zeitgenossen,* ed. Georg Kotowski et al. (Frankfurt a. M., 1965); *Deutsche Sozialgeschichte: Dokumente und Skizzen.* II: 1870-1914, ed. Gerhard A. Ritter and Jürgen Kocka (Munich, 1974); Friedrich-Wilhelm Henning, *Die Industrialisierung in Deutschland 1800 bis 1914* (Paderborn, 1973); Ernst Johann and Jörg Junker, *German Cultural His-*

tory of the Last Hundred Years (Munich, 1970), pp. 9-160; Friedrich Lütge, *Deutsche Sozial- und Wirtschaftsgeschichte* (Berlin, 1966), pp. 503-532; Golo Mann, *The History of Germany since 1789* (London, 1968), pp. 199-418; Golo Mann, "The Second German Empire: The Reich that Never Was," in *Upheaval and Continuity: A Century of German History,* ed. E. J. Feuchtwanger (Pittsburgh, 1974), pp. 29-46; Roy Pascal, *From Naturalism to Expressionism: German Literature and Society 1880-1918* (New York, 1973); J. C. G. Rohl, *Germany without Bismarck: The Crisis of Government in the Second Reich, 1890-1900* (London, 1967); Arthur Rosenberg, *The Birth of the German Republic: 1871-1918* (New York, 1962); Arthur Rosenberg, *The History of the Weimar Republic* (London, 1936); A. J. Ryder, *Twentiety-Century Germany: From Bismarck to Brandt* (New York, 1973), pp. 1-281; Stearns.

3. Nietzsche's influence on Expressionism will be discussed in Chapter 4. For a measure of his importance for this movement, see Gottfried Benn's glowing tribute to him: "Nietzsche — Nach fünfzig Jahren," rpt. in Gottfried Benn, *Gesammelte Werke,* ed. Dieter Wellershoff (Wiesbaden, 1962), pp. 482-93.

4. Walter Kaufmann, "Introduction," *The Portable Nietzsche,* ed. Walter Kaufmann (New York, 1968), p. 16.

5. Friedrich Nietzsche, *Die fröhliche Wissenschaft,* in *Werke,* II, ed. Karl Schlechta (Munich, 1966), p. 127.

6. See, for example, Thomas Mann's tribute to Freud, "Freud and the Future," in *Essays of Three Decades,* trans. H. T. Lowe-Porter (New York, 1948), pp. 411-28, particularly p. 427.

7. Sigmund Freud, *The New Introductory Lectures on Psychoanalysis,* trans. W.J.H. Sprott (New York, 1933), p. 105.

8. *The Basic Writings of Sigmund Freud,* trans. and ed. by Dr. A. A. Brill (New York, 1938), p. 510. Just prior to the beginning of Expressionism, Freud and other psychologists noted a marked trend in contemporary Europeans towards a growing nervousness. Freud traced it to sexual frustration under an increasingly demanding and repressive society. See Sigmund Freud, " 'Civilized' Sexual Morality and Modern Nervousness," (orig. pub. in 1908) in Sigmund Freud, *The Complete Psychological Works,* ed. by James Strachey, vol. IX (London, 1959), pp. 181-204.

9. This is the general mood of the ruling classes, recorded by contemporaries who have chronicled the era and have therefore referred to it as "the golden age," "the age of our innocence," "the good old days," "the age of security." These chroniclers are cited and discussed in Allen, *Literary Life,* pp. 27ff. See there also footnotes 3 and 4, pp. 556-7.

10. Cited in Ryder, p. 92.

11. *Loc. cit.*

12. Pascal, p. 8.

13. The phrase "our place in the sun" ("unser Platz an der Sonne") was coined by Bernhard von Bülow, Chancellor from 1900-09, in a speech

before parliament in 1897 on Germany's policy in the Far East. See *Historisches Lesebuch*, II: 1871-1914, ed. Gerhard A. Ritter (Frankfurt a. M. and Hamburg, 1967), p. 301.

14. Lütge, pp. 506-07.

15. For a typical Expressionist response to this problem see Franz Pfemfert, "Im Zeichen der Schülerselbstmorde," *Die Aktion,* I (1911), cols. 257–58.

Chapter Four

1. Ludwig Meidner, "Erinnerung an Dresden," rpt. in *Expressionismus: Aufzeichnungen,* ed. Raabe, p. 149. This memoir was first published in *1918: Neue Blätter für Kunst und Dichtung* I (1918), pp. 36-38.

2. Ernst Wilhelm Lotz, *Wolkenüberflaggt: Gedichte,* Der jüngste Tag, no. 36 (Leipzig, 1916).

3. Henny Lotz, "Nachwort," Ibid., p. 57.

4. Wolfgang Rothe, "Einleitung," *Deutsche Grossstadtlyrik vom Naturalismus bis zur Gegenwart,* ed. Wolfgang Rothe (Stuttgart, 1973), p. 13.

5. See Allen, *Literary,* pp. 118ff.

6. Kurt Hiller, "Begegnungen mit 'Expressionisten,'" in *Expressionismus: Aufzeichnungen,* ed. Raabe, p. 27

7. Kurt Hiller, *Die Weisheit der Langenweile,* I (Leipzig, 1913), pp. 116-19.

8. *Ibid.,* p. 119.

9. *Ibid.,* pp. 134-37.

10. *Der Kondor,* ed. Kurt Hiller (Heidelberg, 1912).

11. Ernst Blass, *Die Strassen komme ich entlang geweht* (Heidelberg, 1912), p. 29.

12. Arthur Silbergleit, "Die Stimme der Stadt," *Die Aktion* I (1911), columns 565-66.

13. Ludwig Meidner, "Anleitung zum Malen von Grossstadtbildern," rpt. in Paul Pörtner, *Literatur-Revolution 1910-1925,* II (Neuwied a. R. and Berlin-Spandau, 1961), pp. 164-65.

14. Oskar Kanehl, "Tagebuchblatt," *Wiecker Bote* I, (1913), p. 16.

15. Berthold Viertel, "Die Stadt," in Berthold Viertel, *Die Spur,* Der jüngste Tag, no. 13 (Leipzig, 1913), p. 22.

16. Johannes R. Becher, "Die Stadt der Qual" and "Berlin," in Johannes R. Becher, *Verfall und Triumph,* vol. II (Berlin, 1914), pp. 118-29, 141-44; Martin Gumpert, "Eroberte Stadt," in Martin Gumpert, *Verkettung: Gedichte, Der jüngste Tag,* no. 38 (Leipzig, 1917), p. 18; Ernst Blass, *Die Strassen komme ich entlang geweht;* Walter Rheiner, "Mann," rpt. in Rothe, p. 180.

17. George Heym, *Dichtungen und Schriften, I: Lyrik,* ed. Karl Ludwig Schneider et al. (Hamburg and Munich, 1964), pp. 186–87, 192, 220–26.

18. Albert Ehrenstein, "Wien," in Albert Ehrenstein, *Gedichte und Prosa,* ed. Karl Otten (Neuwied a.R. and Berlin-Spandau, 1961), p. 178.

19. Cited by Otten in his memoir on Macke's circle in Bonn in 1914: Karl Otten, "1914 — Sommer ohne Herbst: Erinnerung an August Macke und die Rheinischen Expressionisten," in *Expressionismus: Aufzeichnungen,* ed. Raabe, p. 152. "Maria im Kapitol" ("Maria in the Capitol") is the name of an early medieval church in Cologne, which rests on the site of an earlier Roman temple dedicated to the Capitoline divinities. The "Madonna mit Wickenblüte" ("Madonna with Vetch Blossom") is the central section of a triptych now owned by the Wallraf-Richartz-Museum in Cologne; it is dated ca. 1410–40 and is by an unidentified Northwest German master.

20. Brod's German is "die Generation des Trotzdem." See Max Brod, *Streitbares Leben: 1884-1968* (Munich, Berlin, Vienna, 1969), pp. 241 ff. For a similar view see Willy Haas, *Die literarische Welt* (Munich, 1957), p. 28.

21. Erwin Loewenson, *Georg Heym oder vom Geist des Schicksals* (Hamburg, Munich, 1962), p. 65.

22. Cited after the version in *Menschheitsdämmerung,* ed. Pinthus, p. 39. The exact date of composition is uncertain. It was first published in the January 11, 1911 issue of *Der Demokrat,* III (1911), column 43. Hiller states in "Begegnungen mit 'Expressionisten,' " a memoir included in *Expressionismus: Aufzeichnungen,* ed. Raabe, pp. 24-35, that he knew the poem "long before Franz Pfemfert published it" in *Der Demokrat.* This is also the assumption of Armin Arnold, "Ist der Halleysche Komet am Expressionismus schuld? Eine Klärung der Missverständnisse um Jakob van Hoddis' Gedicht 'Weltende,' " *Neue Zürcher Zeitung* (November 29, 1970), no. 556 of the foreign edition, pp. 51-52. Arnold maintains that Hoddis's poem was merely a satire on the public fears at the predicted approach of Halley's Comet to the earth in May, 1910. While we must agree that such fears may very well have inspired this poem, Arnold's interpretation by no means either explains all of its aspects or the profound impact it had on its readers. I will discuss this poem, the imitations of it by other Expressionists and its impact on its readers in Chapters 5 and 6.

23. Carl Sternheim, "Gedanken über das Wesen des Dramas," rpt. in Carl Sternheim, *Gesamtwerk,* VI, ed. Wilhelm Emrich (Neuwied a.R., Berlin, 1966), p. 19.

24. Rudolf Kurtz, "Programmatisches," *Der Sturm,* I (1910), p. 2.

25. Stadler, *Dichtungen,* I., p. 127.

26. Heinrich Mann, "Geist und Tat," *Pan,* I (1911), pp. 137-43.

27. Arthur Kronfeld, "Klassizität als Forderung," *Die Argonauten,* I (1914), p. 214. Iwan Goll declared in a 1914 manifesto: "[Expressionism] rejects the aesthetics of 'l'art pour l'art, for it is less a form of art than a form of experience." Iwan Goll, "Expressionismus," rpt. in Pörtner, II, p. 177.

28. Kandinsky, *Concerning the Spiritual in Art,* pp. 10-26 and ff.

29. *Menschheitsdämmerung,* ed. Pinthus, p. 23.

30. Kasimir Edschmid, "Über den dichterischen Expressionismus," in Edschmid, *Über den Expressionismus,* pp. 48ff. Another important summary manifesto by Edschmid is "Über die dichterische deutsche Jugend," *ibid.,* pp. 12-32.

31. Kurt Hiller, "Ortsbestimmung des Aktivismus," rpt. in Pörtner, II, p. 433.

32. Ludwig Rubiner, *Der Mensch in der Mitte* (Berlin-Wilmersdorf, 1917), pp. 7, 18.

33. Stadler, *Dichtungen,* I, p. 110.

34. *Kameraden der Menschheit: Dichtungen zur Weltrevolution,* ed. Ludwig Rubiner (Potsdam, 1919).

35. Cited after the rpt. (Leipzig, 1971), p. 167.

36. Rubiner's anthology prints only an abbreviated version of the poem, *ibid.,* p. 43. I cite from the original version in Johannes R. Becher, *An Europa: Neue Gedichte* (Leipzig, 1916), p. 1, where it bears the title (given in the index only) "Eingang."

37. Theodor Däubler, *Der neue Standpunkt* (Dresden-Hellerau, 1916), p. 137.

38. Edschmid, "Über den dichterischen Expressionismus," p. 54.

39. Pinthus, "Zur jüngsten Dichtung," p. 72.

40. René Schickele, "Wie verhält es sich mit dem Expressionismus?" rpt. *Expressionismus: Der Kampf,* ed. Raabe, p. 178. Originally published in 1920 in *Die Weissen Blätter,* VII (1920), pp. 337-40.

41. Gottfried Benn, "Querschnitt," rpt. in Gottfried Benn, *Gesammelte Werke,* II, ed. Dieter Wellershoff (Wiesbaden, 1962), p. 467; "Sanger" and "Meer- und Wandersagen." rpt. in *ibid.,* III (1963), pp. 59, 67; and "Doppelleben," rpt. in *ibid.,* IV (1961), p. 138.

42. Many Expressionists have reported that sexuality and the question of sexual fulfillment were the central issues of their generation: Stefan Zweig, *Die Welt von gestern* (Stockholm, 1944), pp. 88-89; Richard Seewald, *Der Mann von gegenüber: Spiegelbild eines Lebens* (Munich, 1963), pp. 63 ff; *Ego und Eros: Meistererzählungen des Expressionismus,* ed. Karl Otten (Stuttgart, 1963), p. 547; Willy Haas, pp. 28-29.

43. Gottfried Benn, "Das moderne Ich," rpt. in Benn, *Gesammelte Werke,* I (1962), pp. 7-22.

44. Gottfried Benn, "Einleitung," *Lyrik des expressionistischen Jahrzehnts,* ed. Gottfried Benn (Wiesbaden, 1955), p. 11.

45. Pinthus, "Zur jüngsten Dichtung," p. 77.

46. Oskar Maria Graf, *Wir sind Gefangene: Ein Bekenntnis aus diesem Jahrzehnt* (Munich, 1927), p. 112.

47. Alfred Döblin, "An Romanautoren und ihre Kritiker: Berliner Programm," rpt. Pörtner, I, p. 283.

48. Paul Kornfeld, "Der beseelte und der psychologische Mensch,"

Das junge Deutschland I (1918), pp. 1-13.

49. Edschmid, "Über den dichterischen Expressionismus," pp. 60-63.

50. Döblin, "An Romanautoren und ihre Kritiker," p. 284.

51. Max Picard, "Expressionismus," rpt. in *Theorie des Expressionismus,* ed. Otto F. Best (Stuttgart, 1976), pp. 77-78.

52. Pinthus, "Zur jüngsten Dichtung," pp. 68 ff; Carl Einstein, "Totalität," *Die Aktion,* IV (1914), columns 345-47. A very similar position is taken by many other Expressionists, without using the same label: Döblin, "An Romanautoren und ihre Kritiker," p. 284; Edschmid, "Über die dichterische deutsche Jugend," in Edschmid, *Über den Expressionismus,* pp. 23-26; Edschmid, "Über den dichterischen Expressionismus," pp. 48-49, 51-52, 55, 58, 62, 63; Loewenson, pp. 60-61.

53. Carl Sternheim, "Das gerettete Bürgertum," *Gesamtwerk,* VI, pp. 45-47; Carl Sternheim, "Die unbescholtene Mannigfaltigkeit," *ibid.,* pp. 99-100.

54. Edschmid, "Über die dichterische deutsche Jugend," pp. 51-52; Edschmid, "Über den dichterischen Expressionismus," pp. 56-64.

55. Herwarth Walden, "Das Begriffliche in der Dichtung," rpt. in Pörtner, I, p. 411; Lothar Schreyer, "Expressionistische Dichtung," rpt. *ibid.,* pp. 436-37, 442-43; Lothar Schreyer, "Das Drama," rpt. *ibid.,* p. 433; Rudolf Blümner, "August Stramm," rpt. *ibid.,* pp. 450-53; Kurt Schwitters, "Selbstbestimmungsrecht der Künstler," rpt. *ibid.,* pp. 453-54; Otto Nebel, "Vorworte zur Dichtung UNFEIG," rpt. *ibid.,* p. 457; Kurt Liebmann, "August Stramm," rpt. *ibid.,* p. 430.

56. Heinrich Vogeler-Worpswede, *Über den Expressionismus der Liebe: Der Weg zum Frieden,* Die Silbergäule, no. 12 (Hannover, 1919), pp. 10-12.

57. Otto Gross, "Zur Überwindung der kulturellen Krise," *Die Aktion,* III (1913), column 384.

58. The term "dialectical monism" as a summary label for the central ideal in Nietzsche's philosophy is taken from Walter Kaufmann, *Nietzsche: Philosopher, Psychologist, Antichrist* (Princeton, 1974), pp. 128-31, 235-46.

59. Benn, "Nietzsche — Nach fünfzig Jahren," p. 482. See footnote 3 of Chapter Three above. The English translation is quoted after *Twenty German Poets,* ed., trans. and introduced by Walter Kaufmann (New York, 1962), p. 263. See also Benn, "Einleitung," *Lyrik des expressionistischen Jahrzehnts,* p. 12.

60. Friedrich Nietzsche, *Die Geburt der Tragödie aus dem Geiste der Musik,* in *Werke,* I, ed. Karl Schlechta (Munich, 1966), especially pp. 113-34; Kaufmann, *Nietzsche,* pp. 178ff.

61. Loewenson, *Georg Heym,* p. 61. For similar statements of position in the same circle see Erich Unger, "Vom Pathos," *Der Sturm,* I (1910), p. 316; Erich Unger, "Nietzsche," *Der Sturm,* I (1911), p. 380; Ernst Blass, "Vor-Worte," in Blass, *Die Strassen komme ich entlang geweht,* pp. 3-8;

Ernst Blass, "Vor-Worte" (the programmatic speech which opened the first meeting of the cabaret "Gnu" in Berlin on November 2, 1911), *Herder-Blätter,* I, no. 3 (1913), pp. 49-50. Hiller's related view is discussed below.

62. Kurt Hiller, "Über Kultur," in Hiller, *Die Weisheit der Langenweile,* pp. 56, 63.

63. Else Lasker-Schüler, *Gesammelte Werke,* I, ed. Friedhelm Kemp (Munich, 1959), p. 164.

64. Anselm Ruest, "Apollodoros: Über Lyrik ein Dialog," *Die Bücherei Maiandros,* III (1913), pp. 1-38.

65. *Ibid.,* p. 3. Edschmid states this same kind of ideal in terms of a fusion of "Geist" ("spirit, mind") and "Blut" ("Blood"). See Edschmid, "Über die dichterische deutsche Jugend," pp. 31-32.

66. *Ibid.,* p. 37.

67. Benn, "Das moderne Ich," p. 8.

68. *Ibid.,* pp. 7-22. See also Gottfried Benn, "Epilog und lyrisches Ich," rpt. in *Gesammelte Werke,* IV, pp. 7-14.

69. Meidner, "Erinnerung an Dresden," p. 146.

70. Wallace Stevens, "Adagia," in Wallace Stevens, *Opus Posthumous,* ed. Samuel French Morse (New York, 1957), p. 158. Stevens (1879-1955) is an appropriate American poet to cite in the context of Expressionism, since he has much in common with the philosophy of that contemporaneous movement. His poem "Of Mere Being," for example, parallels Expressionism in its attempt to point to the primary physical essense of existence, unbounded by the norms of time and space. See Wallace Stevens *The Palm at the End of the Mind* (New York, 1971), p. 398.

71. Stefan Zweig, "Das neue Pathos," rpt. *Expressionismus: Der Kampf,* ed. Raabe, pp. 15-22.

72. Kenneth Rexroth, *American Poetry in the Twentieth Century* (New York, 1971), p. 141. The intimate parallels between German Expressionism and the American Beat movement are fascinating: e.g., the return to the model of Walt Whitman, the intense concern with tangible contemporary existence, opposition to excessive materialism, the search for essential being, the emphasis on spiritual values, the assumption of moral responsibility for the contemporary world, the eventual politicization of the movement under the impact of socialist and communist ideas, etc.

73. Blass, "Vor-Worte," in Blass, *Die Strassen komme ich entlang geweht,* p. 4.

74. Leonhard Frank, *Links wo das Herz ist* (Munich, 1967), pp. 63-64; See Allen, *Literary,* pp. 53 ff., 148 ff.

75. Max Krell, *Das alles gab es einmal* (Frankfurt a.M., 1961), p. 48; Else Lasker-Schüler, *Lieber gestreifter Tiger: Briefe von Else Lasker-Schüler,* I, ed. Margarete Kupper (Munich, 1969), p. 67; Hans Purrmann, "Erinnerungen an den Maler Rudolf Levy und an die mit ihm verlebten Jahre der Freundschaft," in Rudolf Levy, *Bildnisse, Stilleben, Land-*

schaften (Baden-Baden, 1961), p. 40; Wolfgang Goetz, *Im 'Grössen-wahn,' bei Pschorr und anderswo...Erinnerungen an Berliner Stamm-tische* (Berlin, 1936), p. 14.

76. Frank, *Links,* p. 64.

77. Seewald, *Der Mann von gegenüber,* pp. 85-86.

78. The German strain of Dadaism, which first appeared in Zurich and was then exported to Berlin at the end of the war, was an offshoot of Expressionism, both as far as the sources of its adherents — all of whom were Expressionists — and the nature of its forms and ideas were concerned. There were no significant differences between the program and poetry of Dadaism and those of Expressionism. For a more detailed treatment of Dadaism and its relationship to Expressionism see Allen, *Literary,* pp. 505-53.

79. For a more thorough list of these publications See Paul Raabe, *Die Zeitschriften und Sammlungen des literarischen Expressionismus: Repertorium der Zeitschriften, Jahrbücher, Anthologien, Sammelwerke, Schriftenreihen und Almanache 1910-1921* (Stuttgart, 1964), pp. 163-97.

80. *Ibid.,* pp. 133-50.

81. *Die Aktion,* IV (1914), column 320.

82. Rudolf Kayser, "Literatur in Berlin," rpt. in *Expressionismus: Der Kampf,* ed. Raabe, p. 130. This early historical summary of the origins of Expressionism was first published in 1918 in *Das junge Deutschland,* I (1918), pp. 41-42.

83. Carl Zuckmayer, *Als wär's ein Stück von mir: Horen der Freundschaft* (Vienna, 1966), p. 198.

Chapter Five

1. See Armin Arnold, *Die Literatur des Expressionismus: Sprachliche und thematische Quellen* (Stuttgart, Berlin, Cologne, Mainz, 1966), pp. 9-56.

2. *Ibid.,* p. 55.

3. E.g., several of Stramm's plays, such as *Sancta Susanna (Saint Susanna,* 1914) and *Rudimentär (Rudimentary,* 1914), include roles in north German dialects; parts of Lasker-Schüler's play *Die Wupper (The Wupper,* 1909) are in the dialect of the Wupper valley; and Benn's poem "Fleisch" ("Flesh," 1917) makes wide use of Berlin dialect. See August Stramm, *Das Werk,* ed. René Radrizzani (Wiesbaden, 1963), pp. 131-64; Else Lasker-Schüler, *Gesammelte Werke,* II, pp. 973-1056; Benn, *Gesammelte Werke,* III, pp. 33-38.

4. *Menschheitsdämmerung,* ed. Pinthus, p. 47.

5. See Franz Pfemfert's note, expressing the same opinion, in *Die Aktion,* III (1913), column 942. Other noted imitations of Hoddis's poem include Becher's "Gesang vor Morgen," in Johannes R. Becher, *Verfall*

und Triumph (Berlin, 1914), p. 16; Heym's "Umbra vitae," in *Menschheitsdämmerung,* ed. Pinthus, pp. 39–40; Lichtenstein's "Nebel," ibid., p. 59; Boldt's "Die Sintflut," in Paul Boldt, *Junge Pferde! Junge Pferde!* (Leipzig, 1914), p. 13; Hardekopf's "Spät," in Ferdinand Hardekopf, *Privatgedichte* (Munich, 1921), p. 32; Trakl's "Trübsinn," in Georg Trakl, *Dichtungen und Briefe,* ed. Walther Killy and Hans Scklenar (Salzburg, 1969), vol. 1, p. 53.

6. Lichtenstein suggests in his own, short explication of the poem that this effect was, indeed, consciously intended. See Alfred Lichtenstein, "Die Verse des Alfred Lichtenstein," *Die Aktion,* III (1913), columns 942–44.

7. This technique is sometimes referred to as "Simultaneity," i.e., direct and simultaneous juxtaposition, without causal connection, of ideas, phenomena, or events normally separated by time and space. It is a technique which pervades not only much of Expressionism, but much of modern, post-1910 Western literature. In Expressionism, it is associated with the desire to overcome divisions of life and widen the scope of experience and vision. Benn and Becher make especially frequent use of the technique. See Benn's poem "Der Sänger," cited later in this chapter, and Becher's "Aufruf zum Neuen Mensch," cited in section V of Chapter 4. Outside Germany, prominent practitioners of "Simultaneity" in this period include Guillaume Apollinaire (see esp. his famous "Zone" in *Alcools: Poémes 1898-1913,* first published in 1913), Ezra Pound (see esp. *The Cantos,* 1917 ff.) and T. S. Eliot (see esp. *The Waste Land,* 1922). In a contemporary review of Joyce's opus, Eliot called the technique "the mythical method." See T. S. Eliot, "Ulysses, Order and Myth," *The Dial* LXXV (Nov., 1923), no. 5, pp. 480–483 and David Perkins, *A History of Modern Poetry* (Cambridge, 1976), pp. 505 ff. Apollinaire's "Zone" was published in *Der Sturm* in the original French in April, 1913; *Der Sturm,* IV (1913), pp. 4–5. It was translated into German by Fritz Max Cahén of the Alfred Richard Meyer circle, shortly after Cahén's return from Paris to Berlin, and published in Meyer's "Lyrische Flugblätter" in November, 1913. See Raabe, *Die Zeitschriften,* p. 165. The Italian Futurists also theorized about the technique. See Umberto Boccioni, "Simultanéité futuriste," *Der Sturm,* IV (1913), p. 151; F. T. Marinetti, "Destruction of Syntax — Imagination without Strings — Words-in-Freedom," a 1913 manifesto rpt. in English translation in *Futurist Manifestos,* ed. Umbro Apollonio (New York, 1973), pp. 105–06. "Simultaneity" is also central to the painting of the period, most conspicuously so in Robert Delaunay's "Tour Eiffel" (1910–11; Folkwang Museum Essen) in which the term itself is scrawled across the canvas.

8. See Hugo Friedrich, *Die Struktur der modernen Lyrik: Von der Mitte des neunzehnten bis zur Mitte des zwanzigsten Jahrhunderts* (Hamburg, 1967), pp. 35–94; Grimm and Schmidt, "Foreign Influences on German Expressionist Poetry," pp. 69–78. Influential translations of Baude-

laire and Rimbaud appeared in 1901 (by Stefan George) and 1906–07 (by K. L. Ammer-Karl Klammer), respectively.

9. *Menschheitsdämmerung,* ed. Pinthus, p. 108. On this motif in German poetry see Bernhard Blume, "Das ertrunkene Mädehen: Rimbauds Ophélie und die deutsche Literatur," *Germanisch-Romanische Monatsschrift* XXXV (1954), pp. 108–119.

10. *Ibid.,* pp. 42–43.

11. This definition is based in part on Ezra Pound's definition of the very closely related technique of the Imagists in England in the same period; see F.S. Flint, "Imagisme," *Poetry: A Magazine of Verse* I (1913), pp. 198-200; Ezra Pound, "A Few Don'ts by an Imagiste," *ibid.,* pp. 200-06.

12. *Menschheitsdämmerung,* p. 65. On Trakl's extensively researched relationship to Rimbaud see Bernhard Böschenstein, "Wirkungen des französischen Symbolismus auf die deutsche Lyrik der Jahrhundertwende," *Euphorion* LVIII (1964), pp. 386ff; Ludwig Dietz, *Die lyrische Form Georg Trakls* (Salzburg, 1959), pp. 97–101; Reinhold Grimm, "Georg Trakls Verhältnis zu Rimbaud," *Germanisch-Romanische Manatsschrift* N.F. IX (1959), pp. 288-315, repr. in *Zur Lyrik-Diskussion,* ed. Reinhold Grimm (Darmstadt, 1966), pp. 271-313; Herbert Lindenberger, "Georg Trakl and Rimbaud: A Study in Influence and Development," *Comparative Literature* X (1958), pp. 21-35; Adolf Menschendörfer, "Trakl und Rimbaud," *Klingsor* II (1925), pp. 93-96; Friedhelm Pamp, "Der Einfluss Rimbauds auf Georg Trakl," *Revue de Littérature Comparée* XXXII (1958), pp. 396-406.

13. A close analysis of the variants to this poem gives strong support to the interpretation given here. See Trakl, *Dichtungen und Briefe,* I, p. 113; II, pp. 185-87. For variations on this theme, all strongly influenced by Nietzsche's concept of the eternal recurrence, see Heym's "Ophelia," discussed above, or the poetry of Benn, Stadler, Zech, and Goll.

14. The use of parallelisms and assonance and alliteration, as opposed to end rhyme and meter, are the dominant rhythmic devices of the poetry of "primitive," "uncivilized" peoples: See Benjamin Roland Lewis, *Creative Poetry: A Study of its Organic Principles* (Stanford, 1931), particularly Chapter III, "The Organic Rhythm of a Poem: Rhythm, The Organic Aspect of All Primitive Emotional Expression," pp. 87-155.

15. See, for example, Carl Sternheim's 1919 essay "Expressionismus und Sprachgewissen," first published posthumously in Sternheim, *Gesamtwerk,* VI, pp. 97-98.

16. On Whitman's influence on Expressionism, see Grimm and Schmidt, "Foreign Influences on German Expressionist Poetry," pp. 70 ff. See also the many Expressionist tributes to him: Benn, "Einleitung," *Lyrik des expressionistischen Jahrzehnts,* p. 8; Ludwig Meidner, "Gruss des Malers an die Dichter" (1920), rpt. in Pörtner, *Literatur-Revolution,* I, p. 113; Zweig, "Das neue Pathos," pp. 17-18; Hiller *Die Weisheit der Langenweile,* p. 130; Arthur Drey's poem "Walt Whitman," *Die Aktion,*

I (1911), column 907. As Grimm and Schmidt point out in the article just cited, Whitman certainly had an important ideological impact on Expressionism, especially with his intense, affectionate concern for mankind and the democratic and socialistic ideals expressed in his poetry. Whitman's poems were published in German translations in several Expressionist publications: *Die Aktion, Die Weissen Blätter, Das Forum, Neue Jugend, Der Friede, Der Ventilator, Menschliche Gedichte im Krieg, Das Kestnerbuch.*

17. See F. T. Marinetti, "Manifest des Futurismus," "Technisches Manifest der Futuristischen Literatur," "Supplement zum technischen Manifest der Futuristischen Literatur," "Tod dem Mondenschein! Zweites Manifest des Futurismus," rpt. in Pörtner, *Literatur-Revolution,* vol. II, pp. 35-41, 47-63, 69-81. English translations are found in *Futurist Manifestos,* ed. Apollonio, pp. 19-24, and F. T. Marinetti, *Selected Writings,* ed. R. W. Flint and trans. by R. W. Flint and Arthur A. Coppotelli (New York, 1972), pp. 39-54, 84-89.

18. *Ibid.,* p. 84.

19. Arnold, *Die Literatur des Expressionismus,* pp. 16-56 and Walter Muschg, *Von Trakl zu Brecht: Dichter des Expressionismus* (Munich, 1963), pp. 58 ff., outline this influence in detail; also Grimm and Schmidt, "Foreign Influences on German Expressionist Poetry," pp. 76-79.

20. Benn, *Gesammelte Werke,* III, pp. 18-19.

21. *Ibid.,* pp. 27-28.

22. *Ibid.,* p. 59.

23. Herwarth Walden, "Arno Holz," "Das Begriffliche in der Dichtung," "Kritik der vorexpressionistischen Dichtung"; Lothar Schreyer, "Expressionistische Dichtung"; Rudolf Blumner, "Die Dichtung als Wortkunst"; all rpt. in Pörtner, *Literatur-Revolution,* I, pp. 395-96, 404-30, 436-46. See the discussions of the "Wortkunst" theory in Allen, *Literary Life,* pp. 236 ff; Richard Brinkmann, " 'Abstrakte' Lyrik im Expressionismus und die Möglichkeit symbolischer Aussage," in *Der deutsche Expressionismus: Formen und Gestalten,* ed. Hans Steffen (Göttingen, 1965), pp. 88-114; Richard Brinkmann, "Zur Wortkunst des Sturm-Kreises," in *Unterscheidung und Bewahrung: Festschrift für Hermann Kunisch,* ed. K. Lazarowicz and W. Kron (Berlin, 1961), pp. 63-78; Arnold, *Die Literatur des Expressionismus,* pp. 28 ff. The term "Wortkunst" was borrowed from Arno Holz, whose poetic experiments also appear to have influenced the *Sturm* poetic theory. See Walden, "Arno Holz," p. 395; Brinkmann, " 'Abstrakte' Lyrik im Expressionismus und die Möglichkeit symbolischer Aussage," p. 96. On the influence of Futurism on the "Wortkunst" theory, see Lothar Schreyer, *Erinnerungen an Sturm und Bauhaus: Was ist des Menschen Bild?* (Munich, 1956), p. 91.

24. Schreyer, "Expressionistische Dichtung," pp. 436–43.

25. See Allen, *Literary Life,* pp. 240 ff.

26. Stramm, *Das Werk,* p. 34.

27. Rudolf Blümner, "Die absolute Dichtung," rpt. in Pörtner, *Literatur-Revolution,* 1, pp. 446-50.

28. Hugo Ball, *Gesammelte Gedichte,* ed. Annemarie Schütt-Hennings (Zurich, 1963), pp. 24-33.

29. Hugo Ball, "Dada Manifesto," trans. Christopher Middleton, in Hugo Ball, *Flight out of Time: A Dada Diary,* ed. John Elderfield (New York, 1974), pp. 219-21.

30. *Ibid.,* p. 71.

31. Ball, *Gesammelte Gedichte,* p. 28. The alienation of the words of this poem from traditional associations was further magnified by a typographically experimental version of it in which each line is printed in a markedly different style of type. See *Dada Gedichte: Dichtungen der Gründer,* ed. Peter Schifferli, et al. (Zurich, 1957), p. 43. The use of visual devices in poetry such as this to produce various effects was also exploited by the English and American Imagists in this period. See Harvey Gross, *Sound and Form in Modern Poetry* (Ann Arbor, 1968), pp. 36-7, 100-129.

32. On "Concrete Poetry" See, e.g., Pierre Garnier, "Jüngste Entwicklung der internationalen Lyrik," in *Zur Lyrik-Diskussion,* ed. Grimm, pp. 451-469; *Theoretische Positionen zur konkreten Poesie,* ed. Thomas Kopfermann (Munich, 1977).

Chapter Six

1. *Menschheitsdämmerung,* ed. Pinthus, p. 80.

2. *Ibid.,* p. 262.

3. Becher, *Verfall und Triumph,* I, pp. 57-62.

4. Benn, *Gesammelte Werke,* III, p. 20.

5. *Expressionismus Lyrik,* ed. Martin Reso et al. (Berlin and Weimar, 1969), pp. 155, 175.

6. *Ibid.,* p. 159.

7. Becher, *Verfall und Triumph,* I, p. 63.

8. Armin T. Wegner, *Das Antlitz der Städte* (Berlin, 1917), p. 66.

9. *Revolution,* (1913), p. 2.

10. Stadler, *Dichtungen,* I, p. 120.

11. Wilhelm Klemm, *Aufforderung: Gesammelte Verse* (Berlin-Wilmersdorf, 1917), p. 67.

12. *Menschheitsdämmerung,* ed. Pinthus, p. 268.

13. *Ibid.,* p. 216.

14. *Deutsche Grossstadtlyrik,* ed. Rothe, p. 133.

15. Oskar Kanehl, *Die Schande: Gedichte eines dienstpflichtigen Soldaten aus der Mordsaison 1914-18* (Berlin-Wilmersdorf, 1922), pp. 28-29.

16. *Ibid.,* p. 30.

17. *Menschheitsdämmerung,* ed. Pinthus, p. 216.

18. *Expressionismus Lyrik,* ed. Reso, p. 515.

19. Becher, *Verfall und Triumph,* I, p. 16.
20. Klemm, *Aufforderung,* p. 105.
21. *Ibid.,* p. 11.
22. *Menschheitsdämmerung,* ed. Pinthus, p. 245.
23. *Ibid.,* p. 224.
24. Lasker-Schüler, *Gesammelte Werke,* I, p. 14.
25. *Ibid.,* p. 288.
26. Benn, *Gesammelte Werke,* III, p. 39.
27. *Ibid.,* p. 57.
28. *Ibid.,* p. 43.
29. *Menschheitsdämmerung,* ed. Pinthus, p. 225, 197-8, 279, 328-9.
30. *Ibid.,* pp. 127-28.
31. Benn, *Gesammelte Werke,* III, p. 25.
32. The dithyramb was originally a Greek "choric hymn, accompanied by mimic gestures, describing the adventures of Dionysus, the god of fertility and procreation." See *Princeton Encyclopedia of Poetry and Poetics,* ed. Alex Preminger et al. (Princeton, 1974), p. 196. It is a form, therefore, which is generally used to express high-pitched excitement and ecstasy; its emotional intensity often results in irregularities in verse and stanzaic structure. Nietzsche established the modern currency of the dithyramb in his "Dionysos-Dithyramben." See Nietzsche, *Werke,* II, pp. 1237-67. Goll was especially fond of the form. See Iwan Goll, *Dithyramben,* Der jüngste Tag, no. 54 (Leipzig, n.d. [1919]), which contains the "dithyrambic" version (1918) of his long, Whitmanesque poem "Der Panama-Kanal": *ibid.,* pp. 33-38.
33. Iwan Goll, *Unter keinem Stern geboren: Ausgewählte Gedichte,* ed. Klaus Schuhmann (Berlin and Weimar, 1971), p. 64.
34. Trakl, *Dichtungen und Briefe,* I, p. 95.
35. Lasker-Schüler, *Gesammelte Werke,* I, p. 155.
36. Stramm, *Das Werk,* p. 32.
37. *Menschheitsdämmerung,* ed. Pinthus, pp. 274-75.
38. Johannes R. Becher, *Gedichte für ein Volk* (Liepzig, 1919), p. 40.
39. Klemm, *Aufforderung,* p. 97.
40. See footnote 52, Chapter Four.

Selected Bibliography

1. Bibliographies and Research Reports

BATT, KURT. "Expressionismus und kein Ende," *Neue deutsche Literatur,* XVII (1969), pp. 173-79.

"Bio-Bibliographischer Anhang zu den Jahrgängen 5-8 (1915-1918)." *Die Aktion: 1915-1918.* Rpt. ed. Paul Raabe. Munich: Cotta and Kösel, II, pp. 4-75.

BRINKMANN, RICHARD. *Expressionismus: Forschungsprobleme 1952-1960.* Referate aus der *Deutschen Vierteljahrsschrift für Literaturwissenschaft und Geistesgeschichte.* Stuttgart: Deutsche Vierteljahrsschrift für Literatur und Geistesgeschichte, 1961. *Expressionismus: Literatur und Kunst 1910-1923: Eine Ausstellung des deutschen Literaturarchivs im Schiller-Nationalmuseum Marbach a.N.* Sonderausstellungen des Schiller-Nationalmuseums, no. 7. Ed. Bernhard Zeller et al. Stuttgart: Langen and Müller, 1960.

Index Expressionismus: Bibliographie der Beiträge in den Zeitschriften und Jahrbüchern des literarischen Expressionismus, 1910-1925. 18 Vols. Nendeln-Liechtenstein: Kraus-Thomson, 1972.

MARTINI, FRITZ. "Deutsche Literatur zwischen 1880 und 1950: Ein Forschungsbericht." *Deutsche Vierteljahrsschrift für Literaturwissenschaft und Geistesgeschichte,* XXVI (1952), pp. 478-535.

PAULSEN, WOLFGANG. "Die deutsche expressionistische Dichtung des 20. Jahrhunderts und ihre Forschung." *Universitas,* XVII (1962), pp. 411-422.

PERKINS, GEOFFREY. *Expressionismus: Eine Bibliographie zeitgenössischer Dokumente 1910-1925.* Zurich: Herbert Lang, 1971.

RAABE, PAUL. *Der späte Expressionismus 1918-1922: Eine Ausstellung der Veranstaltungsreihe "Wege und Gestalten" in der kleinen Galerie, Biberach an der Riss, vom 19. November bis 8. Dezember 1966.* Biberach: Kleine Galerie, 1966.

RAABE, PAUL. "Expressionismus: Eine Literaturübersicht." *Der Deutschunterricht,* XVI (1964), Beilage zu Heft 4.

RAABE, PAUL. *Die Zeitschriften und Sammlungen des literarischen Expressionismus: Repertorium der Zeitschriften, Jahrbücher, Anthologien, Sammelwerke, Schriftenreihen und Almanache: 1910-1921.* Repertorien zur deutschen Literaturgeschichte, no. 1. Stuttgart: Metzler, 1965.

SCHLAWE, FRITZ. *Literarische Zeitschriften: 1885-1933*. Vols. I-II. Stuttgart: Metzler, 1973.

SCHNEIDER, KARL LUDWIG. "Neuere Literatur zur Dichtung des deutschen Expressionismus." *Euphorion,* XLVII (1953), pp. 99-110.

SCHÖFFLER, HEINZ. "Der jüngste Tag: Daten, Deutung, Dokumentation." *Der jüngste Tag: Bücherei einer Epoche.* Rpt., ed. Heinz Schöffler. Vols. I-II. Frankfurt a.M.: Scheffler, 1970.

"Verzeichnis der Mitarbeiter und der Beiträge in den Jahrgängen 1911-1914." *Die Aktion: 1911-1914.* Rpt., ed. Paul Raabe. Stuttgart: Cotta, 1961, pp. 29-112.

2. Collections of Documentary Materials

Briefe der Expressionisten. Ed. Kasimir Edschmid. Frankfurt a. M. and Berlin: Ullstein, 1964.

Der Aktivismus 1915-1920. Ed. Wolfgang Rothe. Munich: Deutscher Taschenbuch Verlag, 1969.

Expressionismus: Aufzeichnungen und Erinnerungen der Zeitgenossen. Ed. Paul Raabe. Olten and Freiburg i.B.: Walter, 1965.

Expressionismus und Dadaismus. Die deutsche Literatur: Ein Abriss in Text und Darstellung, vol. 14. Ed. Otto F. Best. Stuttgart: Reclam, 1974.

Expressionismus: Der Kampf um eine literarische Bewegung. Ed. Paul Raabe. Munich: Deutscher Taschenbuch Verlag, 1965.

Ich schneide die Zeit aus: Expressionismus und Politik in Franz Pfemferts "Aktion": 1911-1918. Ed. Paul Raabe. Munich: Deutscher Taschenbuch Verlag, 1964.

Pörtner, Paul. *Literatur-Revolution: 1910-1925: Dokumente, Manifeste, Programme.* Vols. I-II. Darmstadt, Neuwied a.R. and Berlin-Spandau: Luchterhand, 1960.

Theorie des Expressionismus. Ed. Otto F. Best. Stuttgart: Reclam, 1976.

3. Anthologies of Expressionist Poetry, 1912-32

Der Kondor. Ed. Kurt Hiller. Heidelberg: Richard Weissbach, 1912.

Ballhaus: Ein lyrisches Flugblatt. Lyrische Flugblätter, no. (22). Berlin-Wilmersdorf: Alfred Richard Meyer, 1912.

Neuer Leipziger Parnass. Ed. (Kurt Pinthus). Dem Leipziger Bibliophilenabend zum Jahresessen am 16. November 1912. Leipzig: Poeschel and Trepte, 1912.

Fanale: Gedichte der rheinischen Lyriker R. M. Cahén, J. Th. Kuhlemann, Paul Mayer, Bruno Quandt, Robert R. Schmidt, Paul Zech. Heidelberg: Saturn-Verlag Hermann Meister, 1913.

Der Mistral: Eine lyrische Anthologie. Ed. Alfred Richard Meyer. Berlin-Wilmersdorf: Paul Knorr, 1913.

Die Pforte: Eine Anthologie Wiener Lyrik. Heidelberg: Saturn-Verlag Hermann Meister, 1913.

Der Krieg: Ein Flugblatt. Lyrische Flugblätter, no. (46). Berlin-Wilmersdorf: Meyer, 1914.

1914-1916: Eine Anthologie. Die Aktions-Lyrik, Vol. I. Ed. Franz Pfemfert. Berlin-Wilmersdorf: Verlag der Wochenschrift Die Aktion, 1916.

Sturm-Abende: Ausgewählte Gedichte. Berlin: Verlag Der Sturm, n. d. (1918).

Menschliche Gedichte im Krieg. Europäische Bibliothek, Vol. 3. Zurich: Rascher, 1918.

Lyrisches Bekenntnis: Zeitgedichte. Ed. S. D. Steinberg. Zurich: Rascher, 1918.

Der neue Frauenlob. Lyrische Flugblätter, no. (50). Ed. Alfred Richard Meyer. Berlin-Wilmersdorf: Alfred Richard Meyer, n.d. (1919).

Kameraden der Menschheit: Dichtungen zur Weltrevolution: Eine Sammlung. Ed. Ludwig Rubiner. Potsdam: Kiepenheuer, 1919.

Menschheitsdämmerung: Symphonie jüngster Dichtung. Ed. Kurt Pinthus. Berlin: Rowohlt, 1920. Rpt. Reinbek bei Hamburg: Rowohlt, 1959.

Die Botschaft: Neue Gedichte aus Österreich. Ed. E. A. Rheinhardt. Vienna, Leipzig and Prague: Ed. Strache, n. d. (1920).

Lyrische Dichtung deutscher Juden. Welt-Bücher, vol. 15/16. Welt-Verlag, n. d. (1920).

Verkündigung: Anthologie junger Lyrik. Ed Rudolf Kayser. Munich: Roland-Verlag, 1921.

Verse der Lebenden: Deutsche Lyrik seit 1910. Ed. Heinrich Eduard Jacob. Berlin: Propyläen-Verlag, n. d. (1924).

Expressionistische Dichtungen vom Weltkrieg bis zur Gegenwart. Ed. Herwarth Walden and Peter A. Silbermann. Berlin: Carl Heymann, 1932.

4. Anthologies of Expressionist Poetry, 1948–

MARTINI, FRITZ. *Was war Expressionismus? Deutung und Auswahl seiner Lyrik.* Urach: Port Verlag, 1948.

Lyrik des expressionistischen Jahrzehnts: Von den Wegbereitern bis zum Dada. Intro. by Gottfried Benn. Wiesbaden: Limes, 1955.

Die Lyrik des Expressionismus: Voraussetzungen, Ergebnisse und Grenzen: Nachwirkungen. Ed. Clemens Heselhaus. Tübingen: Niemeyer, 1956.

Gedichte des Expressionismus. Ed. Dietrich Bode. Stuttgart: Reclam, 1966.

Expressionismus Lyrik. Ed. Martin Reso et al. Berlin and Weimar: Aufbau-Verlag, 1969.

131 expressionistische Gedichte. Ed. Peter Rühmkorf. Berlin: Wagenbach, 1976.
Die Lyrik des Expressionismus. Ed. Silvio Vietta. Munich: Deutscher Taschenbuch Verlag/Niemeyer, 1977.

SECONDARY SOURCES

ALLEN, ROY F. *Literary Life in German Expressionism and the Berlin Circles.* Göppingen: Kümmerle, 1974. A Study of the wide-scale congruency and cohesiveness of the multitudinous activities and events in the lives of the Expressionists as they related to literature. Emphasis on the Berlin circles.
ARNOLD, ARMIN. *Die Literatur des Expressionismus: Sprachliche und thematische Quellen.* Stuttgart: Kohlhammer, 1966. An important study of stylistic tendencies (in particular those of the most experimental wing of Expressionism) and thematic elements (especially the "new man") in Expressionist literature.
Aspekte des Expressionismus: Periodisierung, Stil, Gedankenwelt: Die Vorträge des ersten Kolloquiums in Amherst/Massachusetts. Ed. Wolfgang Paulsen. Heidelberg: Stiehm, 1968.
Begriffsbestimmung des literarischen Expressionismus. Ed. Hans Gerd Rötzer. Darmstadt: Wissenschaftliche Buchgesellschaft, 1976. A collection of twenty essays on Expressionism dating from 1934-1972, including several of the most important ones in the history of Expressionist scholarship.
BRINKMANN, RICHARD. "Abstract Lyrics of Expressionism: End or Transformation of the Symbol?" *Literary Symbolism: A Symposium.* Ed. Helmut Rehder. Austin: University of Texas Press, 1965, pp. 109-136.
BRINKMANN, RICHARD. "Zur Wortkunst des Sturm-Kreises: Anmerkungen über Möglichkeiten und Grenzen abstrakter Dichtung." *Unterscheidung und Bewahrung: Festschrift für Hermann Kunisch zum 60. Geburtstag, 27. Oktober 1961.* Berlin: De Gruyter, 1961, pp. 63-78.
BRUGGEN, M. F. E. VAN. *Im Schatten des Nihilismus: Die expressionistische Lyrik im Rahmen und als Ausdruck der geistigen Situation Deutschlands.* Amsterdam: H. J. Paris, 1946. A study of the Expressionist lyric as a manifestation of a nihilistic crisis in German intellectual history and, therewith, as an ideological forerunner of National Socialism.
Der deutsche Expressionismus: Formen und Gestalten. Ed. Hans Steffen. Göttingen: Vandenhoeck and Ruprecht, 1965. A collection of incisive essays on Expressionist literature (emphasis on the poets), painting and music (Schönberg).

Deutsche Literatur im zwanzigsten Jahrhundert: Gestalten und Strukturen. Ed. Hermann Friedmann and Otto Mann. Heidelberg: Rothe, 1955. Symposium volumes on twentieth-century German literature, which includes several essays on individual Expressionists and a summary essay on the movement as a whole.

DUWE, WILLI. *Deutsche Dichtung des 20. Jahrhunderts: Die Geschichte der Ausdruckskunst.* Zürich and Leipzig: Orell Füssli, 1936. An analysis of Expressionist poetry, prose, and drama as a reaction to Naturalism and as part of a rebirth of mysticism and religion in art which began at the turn of the century.

EDSCHMID, KASIMIR. *Lebendiger Expressionismus: Auseinandersetzungen, Gestalten, Erinnerungen.* Vienna, Munich, Basel: Desch, 1961. A major source book on the literary events of the Expressionist movement by one of its former novelists and theorists.

Expressionism as an International Literary Phenomenon. Ed. Ulrich Weisstein. Paris and Budapest: Didier and Akadémai Kiadó, 1973. A collection of twenty-one essays (all in English) on German Expressionism and related tendencies in other Europen countries and America — encompassing literature, music, painting, film, and the theater.

Expressionismus als Literatur: Gesammelte Studien. Ed. Wolfgang Rothe. Bern: Francke, 1969. A considerably expanded, revised, and greatly improved version of the volume originally edited by Friedmann and Mann in 1956 (see below). Besides essays on numerous representative Expressionist poets, dramatists, and novelists and on leading Dadaists, it now also includes several treatments of more general themes, such as Expressionism and society, Expressionism and theology, Expressionism and Impressionism, Expressionism and technology, etc.

Expressionismusdebatte: Materialien zu einer marxistischen Realismuskonzeption. Ed. Hans-Jürgen Schmitt. Frankfurt a.M: Suhrkamp, 1973. A documentary presentation of the debate on Expressionism which was fought out in the late 1930's by exiled writers (Georg Lukács, Klaus Mann, Herwarth Walden, Alfred Kurella, Heinrich Vogeler, et al.) and published mainly in the Moscow-based German exile journal *Das Wort.*

Expressionismus: Gestalten einer literarischen Bewegung. Ed. Hermann Friedmann and Otto Mann. Heidelberg: Rothe, 1956. A symposium volume, which collects essays by scholars on representative poets and dramatists of Expressionism. Includes an introductory chapter on forerunners of the movement (Däubler, Mombert, Otto zur Linde) and an appended essay on Dadaism.

EYKMAN, CHRISTOPH. *Denk- und Stilformen des Expressionismus.* Munich: Francke, 1974.

EYKMAN, CHRISTOPH. *Die Funktion des Hässlichen in der Lyrik Georg Heyms, Georg Trakls und Gottfried Benns: Zur Krise der Wirklichkeitserfahrung im deutschen Expressionismus.* Bonn: Bouvier, 1965.

150 GERMAN EXPRESSIONIST POETRY

150 GERMAN EXPRESSIONIST POETRY

A study of the significance and function of qualities of life traditionally labeled "ugly" in aesthetics. Emphasis on the work of Trakl and Benn. Includes a brief history of the "ugly" in art from Victor Hugo to Naturalism and a lengthy chapter on the concept in Expressionist theoretical writings.

FALK, WALTER. *Leid und Verwandlung: Rilke, Trakl und der Epochenstil des Impressionismus und Expressionismus.* Salzburg: Otto Müller, 1961. A juxtaposition of Impressionism and Expressionism primarily through a comparison of the work of Rilke with that of Kafka and Trakl.

FRIEDRICH, HUGO. *Die Struktur der modernen Lyrik: Von Baudelaire bis zur Gegenwart.* Hamburg: Rowohlt, 1956. A seminal study in the understanding of the decisive heritage of modern poetry in the stylistic innovations of the great nineteenth-century French poets (Baudelaire, Rimbaud, Mallarmé).

GARNIER, ILSE and PIERRE. *L'Expressionisme allemand.* Paris: Silvaire, 1962. The major French survey of German Expressionism.

Gedichte der "Menschheitsdämmerung": Interpretationen expressionistischer Lyrik. Ed. Horst Denkler. Munich: Wilhelm Fink, 1971. A collection of detailed interpretations of the most representative poems in the major anthology of Expressionist poetry. The volume is introduced by a very enlightening essay on the background to the conception and compiling of *Menschheitsdämmerung* by its editor, Kurt Pinthus.

GRUBER, HELMUT. "The political-Ethical Mission of German Expressionism." *The German Quarterly* XI (1967), pp. 186-203.

HAMBURGER, MICHAEL. *Contraries: Studies in German Literature.* New York: Dutton, 1970.

HAMANN, RICHARD and JOST HERMAND. *Expressionismus.* Berlin: Akademie-Verlag, 1975. A comprehensive and penetrating survey of Expressionism in art, literature, and music.

HELELHAUS, CLEMENS. *Deutsche Lyrik der Moderne: Von Nietzsche bis Yvan Goll: Die Rückkehr zur Bildlichkeit der Sprache.* Düsseldorf: Bagel, 1962. Largely a collection of interpretations of individual poems of the modern period, including a substantial sampling of Expressionist lyrics. An insightful and highly original study, which is strongly oriented towards the formal innovations of Expressionism.

Interpretationen expressionistischer Lyrik: Die Menschheitsdämmerung. Ed. "A Collective." Munich: Oldenburg, 1971. An abridged version of the volume of similar title edited by Horst Denkler the same year (see above). Includes a new interpretation of a poem by Lasker-Schüler.

KAUFMANN, HANS. *Krisen und Wandlungen der deutschen Literatur von Wedekind bis Feuchtwanger: Fünfzehn Vorlesungen.* Berlin: Aufbau-Verlag, 1968. Contains a lengthy chapter on the Expressionist lyric and another one on the further development of its distinctive features in post-Expressionist poetry.

KEMPER, HANS-GEORG. *Vom Expressionismus zum Dadaismus: Eine Eiführung in die dadaistische Literatur.* Kronberg Taunus: Scriptor, 1974.

KILLY, WALTHER. *Wandlungen des lyrischen Bildes.* Göttingen: Vandenhoeck and Ruprecht, 1967. A study of the development of poetic imagery from Goethe to Trakl, Benn and the early Brecht.

KLARMANN, ADOLF D. "Expressionism in German Literature: A Retrospective of a Half Century." *Modern Language Quarterly,* XXVI (1965), pp. 62-92.

KNEVELS, WILHELM. *Expressionismus und Religion: Gezeigt an der neuesten deutschen expressionistischen Lyrik.* Tübingen: Mohr, 1927.

KREUELS, ALBERT. *Prophetie und Vision in der Lyrik des deutschen Expressionismus.* Freiburg: Knasiusdruck, 1955.

KRISPYN, EGBERT. *Style and Society in German Literary Expressionism.* Gainesville: University of Florida Press, 1964. A brief, but very informative, sociological study of literary Expressionism. Offers several significant insights into the conditioning factors of Expressionism in its social, political, economic, and philosophical background.

KOLINSKY, EVA. *Engagierter Expressionismus: Politik und Literatur zwischen Weltkrieg und Weimarer Republik.* Stuttgart: Metzler, 1970. A treatment of the politically committed writings of the Expressionists composed at the close of the first World War.

MACLEAN, HUGH. "Expressionism" in *Periods in German Literature.* Ed. James M. Ritchie. London: Wolff, 1966, pp. 257-80.

MAIER, RUDOLF N. *Paradies der Weltlosigkeit: Untersuchungen zur abstrakten Dichtung seit 1909.* Suttgart: Klett, 1964.

MARTENS, GUNTER. *Vitalismus und Expressionismus: Ein Beitrag zur Genese und Deutung expressionistischer Stilstrukturen und Motive.* Stuttgart: Kohlhammer, 1971. Illuminates the close ties between vitalism and Expressionism in literature and philosophy in the work of Nietzsche, Simmel, Bergson, Dehmel, Wedekind, Lasker-Schüler, Schickele, Stadler, Heym, Kaiser.

MAUTZ, KURT. "Die Farbensprache der expressionistischen Lyrik." *Deutsche Vierteljahrsschrift für Literaturwissenschaft und Geistesgeschichte,* XXXI (1957), pp. 465-505.

MEYER, ALFRED RICHARD. *Die maer von der musa expressionistica: Zugleich eine kleine Quasi-Literaturgeschichte mit über 130 praktischen Beispielen.* Düsseldorf-Kaiserwerth: Die Fähre, 1948. The critical memoirs of a former expressionist on the movement which he helped to launch. Contains references to many important facts and aspects of Expressionism long forgotten or overlooked by historians.

MITTNER, LADISLAO. *L'Expressionismo.* Bari: Laterza, 1965. The major Italian survey of Expressionism.

MUSCHG, WALTER. *Von Trakl zu Brecht: Dichter des Expressionismus.* Munich: Piper, 1961. Includes an extensive and very readable introductory essay on Expressionist literature in general as well as several studies of certain of its "major" voices (Trakl, Lasker-Schüler, Döblin, Barlach, et al.).

NEWTON, ROBERT P. *Form in the "Menschheitsdämmerung": A Study of Prosodic Elements and Style in German Expressionist Poetry.* The Hague: Mouton, 1971. A study of the use of traditional prosodic and formal elements in Expressionist poetry as exemplified by the verse in *Menschheitsdämmerung.*

PASCAL, ROY. *From Naturalism to Expressionism: German Literature and Society 1880-1918.* New York: Basic Books, 1973. A sweeping survey of the political, social, economic, and ideological tendencies that informed the era brought to a close by Expressionism and the German November Revolution.

PAULSEN, WOLFGANG. *Expressionismus und Aktivismus: Eine typologische Untersuchung.* Bern and Leipzig: Gotthelf, 1935. A penetrating and very influential study of the metaphysical versus the activist tendencies in Expressionist literature.

PINTHUS, KURT. *Der Zeitgenosse: Literarische Portraits und Kritiken.* Marbach a.N.: Schiller-Gesellschaft, 1971.

RAABE, PAUL. "Der Expressionismus als literarisches Phänomen." *Der Deutschunterricht,* XVII (1965), pp. 5-20.

RAABE, PAUL. "Die Revolte der Dichter: Die frühen Jahre des literarischen Expressionismus, 1910-1914." *Der Monat,* XVI (1964), pp. 86-93.

RASCH, WOLFDIETRICH. "Was ist Expressionismus?" *Akzente,* III (1956), pp. 368-73.

RIEDEL, WALTER E. *Der neue Mensch: Mythos und Wirklichkeit.* Bonn: Bouvier, 1970.

RÖLLEKE, HEINZ. *Die Stadt bei Stadler, Heym und Trakl.* Berlin: Erich Schmidt, 1966.

RÜESCH, JÜRG PETER. *Ophelia: Zum Wandel des lyrischen Bildes im Motiv der "navigatio vitae" bei Arthur Rimbaud und im deutschen Expressionismus.* Zürich: Juris-Verlag, 1964.

SAMUEL, RICHARD and R. HINTON THOMAS. *Expressionism in German Life, Literature and the Theatre (1910-1924).* Rpt. Philadelphia: Saifer, 1971. A general introduction to the basic intellectual and socio-political background, the major themes and stylistic tendencies of Expressionism as manifested in literature and the theater.

SCHIROKAUER, ARNO. "Expressionismus der Lyrik" in Arno Schirokauer, *Germanistische Studien.* Ed. Fritz Strich. Hamburg: Ernst Hauswedell, 1957, pp. 19-117.

SCHNEIDER, FERDINAND JOSEF. *Der expressive Mensch und die deutsche Lyrik der Gegenwart: Geist und Form moderner Dichtung.* Stuttgart: Metzler, 1927. An attempt to define the essential Expressionist approach to life through a study of lyrics of the early phase of the movement, especially in the work of Goll, Heym, Stadler, Werfel.

SCHNEIDER, KARK LUDWIG. *Der bildhafte Ausdruck in den Dichtungen Georg Heyms, Georg Trakls und Ernst Stadlers: Studien zum lyrischen Sprachstil des deutschen Expressionismus.* Heidelberg: Winter, 1968. Representative lyrical poets are analyzed as a means of determining the essential features of the Expressionist metaphor.

SCHNEIDER, KARL LUDWIG. *Zerbrochene Formen: Wort und Bild im Expressionismus.* Hamburg: Hoffmann and Campe, 1967.

SCHUMACHER, ERNST. "Lyrik des Expressionismus." *Neue Deutsche Literatur,* IV (1956), pp. 89-102.

SOERGEL, ALBERT. *Dichtung und Dichter der Zeit: Eine Schilderung der deutschen Literatur der letzten Jahrzehnte: Neue Folge: Im Banne des Expressionismus.* Leipzig: Voigtländer, 1925. In particularly its later, revised version (see next entry), and as much because of its excellent illustrations as for its text, this volume has remained the standard introductory survey of Expressionist literature to the present day.

SOERGEL, ALBERT and CURT HOHOFF. *Dichtung und Dichter der Zeit: Vom Naturalismus bis zur Gegenwart.* Vol. I. Düsseldorf: Bagel, 1963.

SOKEL, WALTER. *The Writer in Extremis: Expressionism in Twentieth-Century German Literature.* Stanford: Stanford University Press, 1959. A penetrating analysis of the relationship of Expressionist literature to modern European intellectual, social, and literary history.

STOLTE, HEINZ. "Über expressionistische Lyrik" in Heinz Stolte, *Kultur und Dichtung: Vier Reden.* Iserlohn: Silvia-Verlag, 1947, pp. 30-52.

STUYVER, WILHELMINA. *Deutsche expressionistische Dichtung im Lichte der Philosophie der Gegenwart.* Amsterdam: H. J. Paris, 1939. A study of the relationship of Expressionist literature to contemporary philosophies, including those of Nietzsche, Dilthey, Bergson, Klages, and Heidegger.

THOMKE, HELLMUT. *Hymnische Dichtung im Expressionismus.* Bern, Munich: Francke, 1972. A study of the "hymnic" verse of Expressionism, i.e., eulogistic verse composed in an elevated style and an ecstatic, inspired, or emotional tone. Emphasis on the work of Stadler and Werfel.

VIETTA, SILVIO and HANS-GEORG KEMPER. *Expressionismus.* Munich: Wilhelm Fink, 1975. An introductory study of literary Expressionism, which can serve as a good summary of all the research to date in the field, while also offering some of its own, new perspectives on the literature.

WILLETT, JOHN. *Expressionism.* New York, Toronto: McGraw-Hill, 1970. A general survey of Expressionism in all the arts and of related tendencies before and after the movement. Excellent as a first introduction to the whole complex of the concept of Expressionism.

ZIEGLER, JÜRGEN. *Form und Subjektivität: Zur Gedichtstruktur im frühen Expressionismus.* Bonn: Bouvier, 1972.

Index
